"It's rare to meet a memoirist who can write about the darkest things without judgment and emotional simplification. Wendy C. Ortiz is that kind of writer, and *Excavation* is a book that's devastating, funny, tough, broken, and achingly clear all at the same time."

—Paul Lisicky, author of *The Burning House* and *Lawnboy*

"A raw, unflinching memoir, beautifully told, *Excavation* is a portrait of all that roils beneath the teenage surface, a reminder of the secrets that any kid might be hiding. Ortiz is a fearless and generous storyteller, peeling back the layers of memory, exploring her parents' alcoholism and her years-long illicit relationship with a teacher, never slipping into the easy traps of sentimentality or self-pity. This is a brave, illuminating book; one that resonates deeply with the teenage girl I once was, and one that saddens me as the mother I am now."

—Cari Luna, author of *The Revolution of Every Day*

"*Excavation* stopped my heart. Its story is vital, cracking open a dialogue about what we keep secret and how those secrets shape our lives. The narrative is direct and unflinching, pulling you, challenging you, the kind of read where you call in sick because ohmygod what happens next; but between those moments, Ortiz hits pause and looks back, allowing the reader to breathe with her, to reflect with her, to "wrestle with ghosts," in language so breathtakingly beautiful, so precise and poetic and true."

—Megan Stielstra, author of *Once I Was Cool*

EXCAVATION

A MEMOIR

WENDY C. ORTIZ

Direct inquiries to: info@futuretensebooks.com

Future Tense Books
P.O. Box 42416
Portland, OR 97242

www.futuretensebooks.com

Excavation: A Memoir/ Wendy C. Ortiz. — 1st ed.

Paperback ISBN: 978-1-892061-70-6
Hardcover ISBN: 978-1-892061-48-5

An essay entitled "Mix Tape," which included
details from this memoir, was previously published
by *The Nervous Breakdown*.

Cover Design by Bryan Coffelt

Interior layout by Mareika Glenn

Cover Photo by Andrea Saenz

Printed in the United States of America

AUTHOR'S NOTE

I've relied on handwritten, detailed journals from the period of time that this memoir covers, as well as my own memory.

Names have been changed, in most cases to protect the privacy of individuals.

1986

SEPTEMBER 1986

The classroom was not his when he first arrived; it was the domain of substitute teachers for the first few weeks until he walked into the room.

I slid into my seat and stifled a groan. There was always the silent exasperation that came with new teachers; the need to learn their likes and dislikes, their mannerisms, and what one had to do for extra credit.

My back pushed into the plastic cradle of the chair. The clock arms twitched in micro-movement. I winced.

The teacher's desk was at an angle that faced our neat rows of desks. A cream-colored built-in cupboard behind the desk stood empty and anonymous, but contained the essence of privacy, space that the teacher would fill with teacherly possessions.

Out the window, across the narrow courtyard, was my homeroom teacher's classroom. Mr. Connell was someone I labeled a *spaz*, whose wackiness and unpredictability is what kept our attention during class. I wrinkled my nose at the assignments Mr. Connell conjured up, but I avidly participated, figuring I'd trust his method of teaching to get me an A, or at the very least, a B.

In front of us, though, was the new guy who'd been hired to take the reins and lead us, the advanced eighth grade English class. I could already imagine the assignments: mundane essays about summer vacation, or what we might do with a million dollars won in the California state lottery. Pen-drawn spirals multiplied on my notebook covers, scribbles in my hardcover textbooks, the middle section pages cluttered with my tiny handwriting, messages for the student who would open it next.

This teacher wore slacks and a collared shirt and tie, with a dark cardigan sweater in place of a blazer. His burgundy loafers, with tassels, gleamed. Only one of my other male teachers dressed this way, and I was reminded that these kinds of clothes didn't occupy a place in my father's closet.

While I walked between classrooms at junior high, my father was in a warehouse, doing math problems, his pencil scratching graph paper before he cut sheets of metal to form ducts and casings. This work didn't require more than t-shirts, corduroys or blue jeans, sometimes a denim apron. My mother, on the other hand, worked with and for suited men. She pushed paper, answered phones with the words, "Data processing, this is Dee," and took smoke breaks off of Sunset Boulevard where she worked on the seventh floor of a city office building.

This teacher started talking to us in a fast and easy fashion, as though we were all old friends and he'd just returned from a weekend jaunt. I watched from my desk, noting his easy demeanor, how he was already joking with Brian, the class jester, and how he made eye contact with Veronica, whose attention I craved from the tip of my black boots to the top of my hair-sprayed bangs.

"Mr. Ivers," he introduced himself, his eyes meeting ours resolutely as he spoke.

His voice boomed as his thick hand composed on the blackboard: *IVERS. ENGLISH.* Chalk dust scattered away from him like an aura. I coolly looked down at my wood-top desk when he turned his attention to us, asked questions about the school, how we were doing this fine afternoon. He offered information about himself, smiling, knocking on desks with his fist, inhaling loudly. I wondered whether I wanted to look up again and watch what was suddenly sounding like fun, kids letting go of their fragile teenage seriousness—the laughter catching, the banter baiting.

I decided to display a disinterest I was learning to perfect. This air of disinterest took the place of thinking about school, or how life with my parents felt raw, wounded. My preferred setting was the Sherman Oaks Galleria, which felt wild and thick with the comings and goings of high school dropouts-turned-punks, their colored hair stiffened with spray, hands outstretched awaiting change. Placing myself just outside their unpredictable orbits, I aligned myself with them, and any group that was already drifting against, or outside of, the margins. This way I would not be central to anything, but could simply observe, absorb.

Mr. Ivers, the man with a tie at the head of the class, joked with us, shared that we were his first real teaching job, but that he was *onto us*, that he could hone in on the teenage mind better than we thought. No one challenged this; it seemed plausible. His entrance to the classroom felt like instant habitation: his very being emitted energy, energy that pushed into the corners of the room, high up into the ceiling, up against the windows, daring us to take our eyes off him and look outside.

As soon as I found myself on the edge of my seat, searching the faces of Jennifer, or Tammy, both of whom were laughing and answering Mr. Ivers's questions, I remembered: *Not interested.* I leaned back into the hard frame of the chair and let my knees splay out just enough to suggest a hint of the "unladylike," as my mother would call such a pose. I twirled my pencil around on the desk and kicked Abigail's desk in front of me, wanting her to join me in an active atmosphere of supreme disinterest.

My eyes were dry and itchy. I pointedly glared at the clock again, for effect. I considered the money in my book bag, what it might buy me if I went to the Galleria later. I didn't want to go home. Or, I wanted to go home to parents who didn't fight, didn't drink, and were just *normal*, even though I wanted to be anything but normal. My palms lay flat, motionless against the cool desktop.

~

English class was in the afternoon.

By that time I had already laughed in homeroom, reapplied eyeliner in front of the bathroom mirror at nutrition break, sulked and scowled at math, and sat slackjawed, taking careless notes through history and science. The catering trucks that served as our only lunch choice if we didn't bring our own had come and gone. It was time to master grammar, read old books, and/or stare at the chalkboard as I silently sang Depeche Mode songs to myself *(People are people, so why should it be, you and I should get along so awfully...)*, waiting for the final bell to ring.

I worked at perfecting the art of sighing: long, loud and heavy; eyes rolled to emphasize a look of non-commitment. A careful pursing of lips and the tap of one black boot on the floor: I punctuated English class often until the day Mr. Ivers assigned us to write one creative paragraph.

One creative paragraph, he said. "Surely you all have papers, pens? Okay, go to it. Five minutes. Yeah, you can shoot hoops, Brian, but can you write? Yeah, a *creative* paragraph. Don't give me summer vacation, or what you'd do with a million bucks. Give me one creative paragraph, on anything your little hearts desire. Yep. Here, paper, pen, do you need a desk? How about a brain? Sorry, can't help you with that. Okay, then, go. Start it up, *start me up...*" His voice dissolved into an obnoxious rendition of a song I recognized as the Rolling Stones.

I sighed in exasperation.

I crossed my legs. My black leggings rubbed against each other.

I tugged a little on the long-sleeved white collared shirt wrapped around my waist, its arms embracing my hips, the buttons just touching my thighs. I stared at my notebook page, and tentatively let the pen touch it.

Then the image formed. Fire, hillsides, disaster.

I ground my pen into the blank paper, curving, sloping, across its face, across and back, across and back, until the paragraph appeared on the page.

Five minutes passed.

"Alright, hand 'em up," Mr. Ivers said. Abigail turned from her seat in front of me to take my paper and shot me a look of *Huh? That's it?* A small sea of papers moved to the front of the class, their surfaces whispering softly against one another. Mr. Ivers collected the papers from the students in the front row, walked back to his desk, and leaned against the edge to read each paper to himself.

There was a titter, then a hush, as we watched him relax into his lean, reading, flipping to the subsequent pages rather swiftly. He grunted, occasionally glancing up to say, "Yeah, right!" looking a bashful student in the eye, or "What the...?" directed at another. There was a strange, bouncy feeling in the air, as if we were forgiven for writing poorly, as if he was amused by our adolescent boredom and our confusion and our young, silly way of life.

When he got to my paper, my throat clenched. I knew it was mine, because I'd starting using recycled paper, a telltale soft brown.

He read my paper and paused, re-reading, until I had to take a breath.

Mr. Ivers looked up at me (*He knows my name?* I think), and asked in a low voice, as if we were the only ones in the room, "Wendy, can I read this out loud?"

My head tilted, nodded softly. *Yes*, I thought to myself, too scared to say it aloud. *Just get it over with.*

The class was quiet. They listened as he read each word slowly, words that formed an image of a fire that charged violently down a hillside to ravage the basin below.

When he finished, he looked up and shook his head.

"Excellent," he said. "This is great work. This is what I asked for. Thank you."

My legs untwisted under my desk. I slouched in my seat, hid a smile, looked down at the haggard little etchings on my desk. I tried not to meet his eyes again that day.

Mr. Ivers placed the papers in a corner of his desk, and turned to begin scrawling notes on the blackboard.

The class pressed on.

My palms were wet and I felt unmoored. I wiped my palms on the shirt that encircled my waist with its flimsy, translucent hug.

FALL
1986

"Open your notebooks," Mr. Ivers ordered, stepping backward from us, his eyes blinking rapidly behind his glasses. I saw a glimmer of a smile, and then a furrowed brow in mock seriousness.

"You're going to use these notebooks to compose journal entries. You'll turn the notebooks in to me once a week, every week. You can write about whatever you want, so long as there's evidence of writing somewhere, somehow, in that notebook. Got it?" He held his elbows. He caught my eye.

"Why don't we take just a little bit of class time to start this gig. Anyone have any questions?" Mr. Ivers began moving past students' desks, throwing out joking comments, lingering with kids who pleaded that they had nothing to write about.

I raised my hand. My eyes followed him, starting with his tie. My eyes crept up his thick neck, ending on the cleft in his chin. I glanced at Abigail, who was busy writing in her notebook. She paused, put her head down on her desk. I bit my lip when suddenly Mr. Ivers's eyes met mine.

"Mr. Ivers? Can you c'mere?" I held my raised elbow in the air as if it was a burden to hold up, as if I was wounded and required assistance.

He lifted his palm to me as he focused on Sheila's question. Sheila whined about the assignment and Mr. Ivers cajoled her into starting with just one sentence. When Sheila's pen met paper, he made his way to my desk. I watched him, the way his mouth opened slightly so that I could see his tongue dart out and touch his lips.

When he came to my desk, I pressed my lips together and hid a smile.

"What am I supposed to write about? Like, anything? We can write about anything?" I let my hand touch the cool of the desktop.

"Yep," he answered, looking at me with raised eyebrows. I noticed beads of sweat on his forehead, which was broad and pale. He started to move on to another raised hand, and my arm shot back in the air, straight, sure.

He turned back to me. "Yes, Wendy? Another question?"

I brought my eyes back to the desk, back to the notebook, away from his small, hazel eyes and amused look. "So like it doesn't have to be specifically about school?" I felt my legs twist up under the desk. I imagined I needed a touch-up to my eye-liner. My lips felt chapped under the coat of bronze lipstick.

"Nope," he answered as he moved away from me, down the aisle between desks. "In fact, I would hope that it has hardly anything to do with school."

I watched his back, the expanse of his gray sweater, and inhaled the almost imperceptible scent of his cologne. He went back to briefly conferencing at students' desks. His words were lost on me as I stared at my notebook, its pages naked, waiting to be split open and attacked with my pen in one fluid motion. Later, after half of the first page was covered and I felt like I was coming up for air, I looked up to find Mr. Ivers's eyes fixed on me, a slight smile on his face, as the class bent over their notebooks.

~

After school, I was waiting for my mom to pick me up. My friend Eva and Mr. Ivers flanked my sides, and I felt the dip into nighttime occur even though it was just nearing four-thirty.

Somehow, someway, I mentioned the novel I was writing.

"You're what? You're writing a book?" he said, hands on his hips. The dimple in his chin was showing, and he waited for my answer. I glanced at Eva. She had taken home my special red binder on different occasions, always returning with praise, wanting to read more. Handwritten on lined paper, it contained pages in the hundreds. My book was being written in bubbles of private time: after watching television and instead of watching television, before sleep, between phone calls to friends, sequestered in my bedroom. I savored my identity as an only child, different from most of my friends. Silence, notebooks and carbon paper were commonplace in my bedroom.

"What are you writing?" my mother asked occasionally, only to receive the same answer every time, "Nothing." My father seemed unaware and uninterested in what I was up to when I sat cross-legged on my bed, door not quite closed, Soft Cell crooning softly out of the stereo speakers.

I flinched, imagining what would happen should my parents ever invade the red binder and read its contents. Looking at Mr. Ivers, I felt a tickle in my groin. I bit my lip, leaned heavily on one leg.

"Yeah, I'm writing a book. Eva's read most of it," I answered.

Eva laughed, a sound that mixed appreciation and something else, something like *Watch out, Wendy*. We both knew what the pages contained. And I knew why she was laughing like that. The moment felt like when I steadily walked the length of a swimming pool that got ever deeper, relishing the moment when my feet would touch nothing.

"Well, what's it about? What's going on? Is it your life story?" he inquired, elbowing me playfully. I looked hard at this man, his tie askew, his ruddy complexion brought out by the afterschool patrolling of campus, and now from the teasing he was giving me. My teeth involuntarily clenched under my closed lips. I was aware of being subtly condescended to.

"No," I retorted. "It's fiction." I paused. "About a girl named Ali Milan. And," *Shit, I think, I'm giving it away,* "her boyfriend." *Make this more innocent-sounding.* "And her family," I added. I felt out of breath. My voice had gotten louder, surer.

"And I never want my parents to read it when it gets published," I said. Mr. Ivers was still smiling at Eva and me.

"Why?" he asked, and I saw a man, for an instant, who was enjoying two young girls that he thought he had something over. I made my move.

"Well," I started, looking sidelong at Eva, whose eyes were open wide, her hand to her mouth to stifle giggles, "because there are parts in it where people are, you know, making out, doing more than that, you know. And. Well. It's in detail."

Eva's face was red. Mr. Ivers took a deep breath.

"My parents probably wouldn't like that, because it's based on personal experience," I lied. My feet suddenly felt hot in my black boots, rooted firmly to the cement.

"Well, get those pages to me! I need something to get my blood racing!" Mr. Ivers bellowed, and we all laughed. I wanted to linger over what he meant by this, but I stood stock-still, even as my knees felt loose and I wanted to flee. He was looking at me expectantly. My face was hot. I started to rifle through my bag.

"I can't be here while you read it," I said. "Here, Eva, show him." I handed her the bulky red binder. My heart pounded and I scurried away as soon as she took the manuscript. I watched them from a discrete spot near the manicured bushes that surrounded the A-frame office. They were leafing through the pages together. I put my hand over my mouth, forgetting the other students nearby.

When I spied my mother arriving in her station wagon to pick me up, I quickly retrieved the red binder from them on my way to her car.

"Hey," Mr. Ivers called out to me as I started to open the door to the car, "I wanna talk to you about that book!" I gritted my teeth even as I smiled, waved, and got inside the car, glad that my mother was not conscious of this last exchange, this exchange that made me shift in my seat the whole way home. I was full from this series of recent events, happy I had something to mull over when I got home, something to write about. Still, in the midst of my excitement, I noted the straight line of my mother's mouth and the wrinkles on her forehead. There was an electric tension buzzing from her. Her sunglasses hid her eyes and I snuck a look at her short skirt, which I disapproved of. The radio blared Erasure, a British band my mom loved, which horrified and sickened me because I loved Erasure. I listened to her talk about hot flashes and stared straight ahead. If she flipped the turn signal and maneuvered into the Dales Market parking lot, I knew that the weekend might be flawed with the smell of vodka, the lull of heavy cigarette smoke, my father escaping the house or retreating to the room where he buried himself in hours of Saturday afternoon sports, a fresh beer within reach. I was suddenly still, muscles tensed in the burgundy passenger seat of her car. My body relaxed just slightly as the car turned away from the market.

Hours later, Eva called to tell me this:

"Mr. Ivers wants you to call him at home. Here's his phone number. So you guys can talk about your book."

I didn't question why my friend had my teacher's phone number. All I could think about was *when*.

It was the beginning of a long weekend. I waited until I had a chance, a perfect opportunity, to call Mr. Ivers, the phone number written in my careful script waiting to be used.

NOVEMBER 9
1986

Sunday afternoon.

I had the courage to use the phone number entrusted to me.

I checked to make sure my mother was busy reading and dozing in the living room. My father was stationed in the TV room, reading a true crime book from the library, ignoring a sporting event on television.

I crept to my bedroom and closed the door.

My toes felt ice cold and I put some thick white socks on and tried to keep from shivering. My room was eternally the coldest or the hottest, depending on the season, and shutting the door only magnified either effect. I closed the window to muffle the sound of the nearby freeway. I pressed the square buttons on my Princess telephone and listened for the ring.

Two and a half hours quickly passed.

I had been talking, laughing, hooting with Mr. Ivers, my eighth grade English teacher. A constant smile on my face threatened to break when my cheek muscles quivered.

We talked about my writing, which he raved about, having read the contents of the red binder, my novel in the making. Films we hadn't seen but wanted to see. Museums he wanted to check out now that he lived in Los Angeles. He talked about his hometown and his ex-girlfriend, the college where they met, my own plans for college. The pros and cons of commercial sporting events (he was for, I was against). Whether (my) eighties music could compare to (his) seventies music. Whether or not I was wasting my time reading Stephen King ("Waste of time," he decided).

I was reeling.

Over an hour into this conversation, this conversation that forced me to listen, reply, and think swiftly to keep up with the speed and flow of it, he used the word "crush."

He said "crush" like I said it in sixth grade when I was talking about Marc Hendricks.

He said, "*you*" like I was the embodiment of some kind of dangerous elixir threatening to seduce him, forcing any control he might have over himself underground.

My teacher was revealing to me, admitting to me, that he had a huge *crush* on me.

He said he wondered what it would be like to have his face between my legs, and I crossed my legs hard, trying to imagine what this must mean, flipping mental pages of *Cosmopolitan* in my head to remember what I had read of oral sex, what it might feel like, and I found myself enjoying the way he growled these desires in my ear. There was a tingle that started on my insides and floated gently to the surface of my skin. The cold of the room no longer made me shiver; my socked feet were banging together silently as if part of a strange dance I couldn't control.

I had only made out with someone a handful of times at that point.

Most recently, there was Cougar, a tall, cute, barely-literate boy of twenty. We plunged into back-to-back weekend romps complete with necking in his El Camino and in the courtyard of the Sherman

Oaks Galleria. This minor fling was already over and done with, though, because I didn't have the freedoms of a twenty-year-old, or even a sixteen-year-old. And I knew nothing of faces between legs—it was like imagining esoteric customs of people in foreign lands, like what I read in social studies class.

I absorbed the sound of Mr. Ivers purring in my ear, because it was peppered with things I did understand. He told me of my beautiful mouth, intense eyes, the way he watched my body at school. I was suddenly privy to the details of an oft-imagined scene that involved him and me, where he was pressing his "hardness" against me and then licking my thighs, then my "clit." These words traveled the phone lines from his apartment in Pasadena, a city where I had not been, to North Hollywood, my parents' house by the Hollywood Freeway. When he asked me to touch myself, I sighed and murmured in the right places, but refrained from laying a hand on myself. I didn't really know if masturbation was a true sin or not. I was thirteen, and this had been a solitary, secret act, not something I wanted to be guided towards by a voice on the phone, though I was intrigued by the intimate details he described.

The conversation was punctuated with his heavy breathing, soft words. I heard intakes of breath, like he was smoking a cigarette and exhaling large amounts of smoke, which was not how I smoked at all. He told me, as if I couldn't already guess, that this was our secret, not to be discussed with anyone, not even my best friend Abigail, and it definitely couldn't be written anywhere, like my journal. *Duh*, I thought, rubbing my hand on the side of my thigh, perched on the edge of my bed. Steeped in the praise he gave my writing and the dormant sexiness he had discovered in me, I half-listened for any movement outside my closed bedroom door, any change in volume of the two television sets my parents employed to help them forget a forgettable weekend. No one was drunk, and it was not likely to happen now, since we made it to the finish line of Sunday. The likelihood of my mother bursting in to slur, "How are you? Is everything okay?" and then lingering until I yelled at her to leave, door slamming, was nil. I hid a sigh of relief, not wanting to sound like I was bored.

I was not bored.

I was over-fucking-whelmed. And then we hung up.

My heart felt like it was hovering somewhere outside me, rocking the room with its beat. This day felt like too much to keep inside my body. My lips were dry and my hands trembled as I opened up my journal, the one hidden between my bed and the wall.

I opened its black folder and my fist touched the yellow legal pad.

I committed Mr. Ivers' words to paper.

I remarked on school events from the Friday before—*LB made me laugh the other day and I may spend next weekend with Abigail if she stops acting like a bitch*—between the verbatim words I heard that afternoon, the words I was hardly able to process without grinning madly, tapping my foot excitedly on the carpet, feeling like I had to pee.

It was Sunday. Mr. Ivers was twenty-eight.

NOTES ON AN EXCAVATION:

OPPORTUNITY SCHOOL 2002–2004

During the years when I lived alone in an apartment in Hollywood, I would wake up early once a week and drive out to the westernmost part of the San Fernando Valley.

In my car I carried a binder with a syllabus, study plan, photocopies of writing prompts and exercises, and a handful of excerpts from books. My little literature-mobile, traversing the punishing traffic, all to get to boys I thought of and spoke of as "my kids."

I turned right at the final stoplight on my journey and parked on the quiet street. Yellow hills were not far in the distance, where I'd driven from. I walked onto school grounds, flicking the metal door handle into place once I was inside.

At this school, anyone could walk out. The boys who went to this school were often here because of impossible home circumstances that pushed them out, or problems with the law or other schools. They had the freedom to decide to stay or go, and I felt an immeasurable sense of relief every week when I arrived and saw the same faces. They hadn't left. They were there for *something*.

The boys lived next door and walked onto the school campus and went to classes. The class I taught was one of their options for ten weeks out of a semester. We would meet in the library, with its posters advising students to READ. We would meet in a classroom, with chalkboards and bulletin boards and desks we pushed together so we could face one another.

I was twenty-nine, thirty years old. These boys were fourteen and fifteen years old.

We read excerpts from books that are considered great literature. We talked about the meanings in the stories, the techniques used. Then we bent over our own papers and wrote stories.

These boys took the task to heart. They often wrote their autobiographies, their memoirs. These were gripping, heart-wrenching, incredible stories—when they weren't pushing the envelope and trying to write out all their sexual experiences in one fell swoop.

There was another place I went, lugging my little totes of books and paper and pens and stories.

This place was juvenile hall, downtown, where I always had to drive past the county morgue.

There was an entirely different system in place. There were guards who looked like ex-military and sort of acted like it. There were convoluted locks and mazes to navigate, and code words to understand in case of emergency. I felt less inclined to call or think of these boys as "my boys," as they circulated in or out enough to make me lose track of names and stories. The oppressiveness of the walls and grounds seemed to seep into our interactions.

And why not? Why should they trust me? I was some stranger, coming in from the outside with ideas and words and papers and imploring eyes. I told them I wanted their stories. That the world needed their stories. Who had told them the world needed their stories before?

Other teachers might have. Other adults. But then the adults would move on, the school year might end, or the kid might be so demolished from dealing with shit at home that the words fell away like dirt through your hands.

When I taught girls at juvenile hall, things were no better. In fact, they might have even been worse. I became educated immediately in how these girls saw me and my every move, because they told me. Watching them "act out" was like revisiting my own teenage years, only one thousand times more intense than I had ever seen or experienced. I couldn't begin to know what these girls had gone through.

Before I was allowed to teach girls at juvenile hall, though, there were the girls at the all-girl "juvenile camp" east of downtown Los Angeles.

Here the girls were in perpetual lockdown. The staff often forgot we were visiting at the same time every week and we came in late through all the layers of locked doors, delayed by red tape.

The girls were often medicated to the hilt. There might be slurring, a little drool, or just silence. Big-eyed silence. We were overseen by someone who they sometimes called "Mother." I tried to overlook this arrangement, this surreal circumstance, and "get to work" with them, asking them to read aloud *this*, consider writing *that*.

We brought our medium-sized satchels of hope—writing prompts, passages someone picked out for us to teach.

When they wrote, their stories were unlike anything I'd ever heard. At our final reading, I left somewhat devastated. It was like a long, burning blood draw. I willed my body to not tremble, not cry, because I thought it best not to do so in their presence.

I was twenty-nine, thirty, thirty-one. The girls were thirteen, fourteen, fifteen.

There were moments when I was alone in my apartment that I found myself despairing over stories I'd heard from my students, these girls and boys I'd come into contact with. And there were moments when I remembered: *we are almost the same age difference as I was when I met and studied under Jeff.*

Nausea. In those moments I coughed, gagged on my cigarette, stared out the window some more.

Could I ever imagine having some kind of sexual relationship with these kids, kids who had found themselves in the intimate space of sharing and writing their stories?

Absofuckinglutelynot.

The fact that this question even had to rise, bubble up in me, made me angry. I might never have come up with such a question had it not been my own experience. The story I carried would never be shared with any of the kids I taught, because they had their own traumas to lance, drain, to exorcise.

I asked myself these questions to place the greatest distance between me and Jeff as I could. And it worked like a charm.

1986

At thirteen, I harbored strange and beautiful conditions in the landscape of my body. Like fast-moving weather patterns, I could be embraced by a storm of arousal, experience an onslaught of brush fires that started beneath my skin and ended in a brief rush of rain, all behind my closed bedroom door, pressed against the yellow carpeted floor, panting and writhing.

I didn't call it masturbation. It had no name. I pretended this rapture did not exist. I was fresh from my grandmother's warnings and astute enough to figure out that humping the carpet with nude women etched in my mind's eye was, somehow, *wrong*. Just the fact that this act entailed a softly closed door and a deep intake of breath to withhold the revelatory sigh so it did not travel—these things told me that this was an act that must not be named.

Shame lent a soft, tragic hue to each and every fantasy.

To loosen its grip on me, I added men to the images in my head, men who appeared blurry and peripheral to the contours of the imaginary women lovers. I assured myself I was not a lesbian as I watched men and women have some adolescent, groping version of sex behind my eyes.

The fevered rub of hips against floor, the burn of carpet through clothes, the clenching of toes, the heat spreading into, over, around me as I locked my teeth together and shut my eyes tight: then, finally, the women in my head, and the blurry men, disappeared.

∼

Outside the door to my room were my parents.

It was always this way: my mother folded into a comfortable position on the living room sofa, reading. My father in the TV room reading with the television on. Me in my room with the most windows of all the bedrooms, wishing I could get out but with no destination other than a friend's house or the Galleria, or school. There was a comforting stillness to this bookish family I was in, when my parents weren't drinking and my father came home from work on time.

I was brought up on weekly trips to the library. I culled first from the children's books and later the books in the adult section, where I still feared someone would tap me on the back and tell me I wasn't allowed. The books were pleasure boats I could step into when my parents were despicable with drink. They taught me this pastime, gave it to me like a key. I took the books to my room and got lost inside stories so I didn't have to think about the story outside the door, where a man and a woman yelled shitgoddamnfuck, slurring on occasion, slamming doors often, the man often leaving the house (either for the backyard or a bar), the woman appearing at my door, drunk, broken. Her own mother, my grandmother, knew the secret of this family, the vodka in the cupboard under the sink the source of all that was wrong with her daughter.

Early on, I developed ways of dealing with the story I was living in that did not seem to mirror the stories I saw on television or experienced at the homes of friends.

One way to get out of my story was to get into another story, like the stories of Stephen King, which I desperately wanted to jump inside and live in, especially the scariest ones. Another way was to do the things my grandmother told me to do, in order for God to hear our pleas to keep my mother from drinking and my parents from fighting.

In the shadowy duplex that my grandmother lived in, the Bible was King. The Bible was like the American flag in that you could never let it touch the ground. The solemn black book held a sacred space on her crowded little armchair table in the living room. My grandmother's house, as I got older, became less a place of tea parties and pancakes with milky coffee as a treat, and more a place of watching scary movies and memorizing psalms.

My grandmother loved a Christian song and wanted me to learn it well enough to sing it to her. In exchange I got an oversized Michael Jackson "Thriller" button. My grandmother wanted me to recite a psalm by heart. In exchange I got a record, or more commonly as I got older, cassette tapes until those made way for compact discs. I said the psalm inside nightmares I was trapped in, so that the Lord would release me. And it worked for years.

My grandmother read her Bible every day, in Spanish, aloud, but only loud enough so that I heard mumblings, the *Jesus Cristo* refrain more enunciated than anything else. She gave me a Bible of my own, which I kept at her house. I looked at it from time to time, read it with all of its begatbegatbegat. My grandmother wanted me to read the book cover to cover, and I whined and kicked my chair, because it was so boring, I didn't even get it. Somehow I was coerced into a Bible correspondence course at age eleven, with the expectation that the more I did in God's name, the more he might listen to me, to us, working in His name, praying for an end to my mother's alcoholism.

So: I filled out a perforated slip of paper from a Christian magazine with my grandmother's address, and soon, slim paper booklets arrived with lessons and question and answer sheets. The booklets always arrived from southern states, places that seemed exotic. Multiple choice questions regarding the finer points of the Book of Revelation lurked in my head at night after I signed my name and sealed the envelope to send back my answers. I conjured up images of the booklet covers we received in the mailbox: the whore of Babylon riding a many-headed beast, an amalgamation of several animals I'd seen behind fences at the zoo. I fell asleep thinking of the whore's tight scarlet outfit, her crown, the staff she held in an upright hand as the beast underneath reared on its hind legs. I mailed in my answer sheets, got graded by nameless people or a sterile, central computer. I only scored average. There were no records or toys like my grandmother gave me when I memorized a song or a psalm.

At thirteen, I put an end to Bible correspondence courses. God hadn't listened. In fact, I didn't think he paid the slightest bit of attention.

I started to listen less to my grandmother's admonishments about how God felt about how I behaved. I felt watched because she reminded me that He was watching me every moment. Something about who I was when I was in her house and who I was inside myself suddenly did not seem to fit. None of my friends understood why I would give myself over to a hobby like Bible study. No one knew I was asking for favors, wishes, rescue.

In order to match up the unwieldy planes of my life, I decided to do some careful sorting.

In order to listen to the music I wanted to listen to that my grandmother deemed satanic, I had to tune her out.

In order to touch myself quietly and not think about God watching me, I had to set aside the pencils and white paper tests and give myself over to whatever it was that had a hold on me (and it didn't feel satanic, never).

To stay abreast of new videos on MTV, homework, and extra-credit assignments, I needed to let go of the Bible study.

To stay afloat in my parent's house as the undertow threatened to pull me under, to a place where I screamed and cried into pillows so I didn't have to listen to them fighting, I had to let go of Bible study.

In fact, I wanted to let go with a strong, fine flourish; a flick of my wrist, to send the tests soaring up and away.

Sometimes, though, I still listened for an answer to my dilemmas. When my parents' house was quiet, when one of them was passed out on a couch, or I heard a door slam announcing a new silence, I listened.

I heard nothing.

1985-1986

When I was in sixth grade, I begged my father to let me attend Oakcrest Junior High.

I'd gone to Oakcrest since preschool. I wanted to join my friends planning to attend the junior high of the same name, located a bit off of my parents' radar. My father, who still drove me to school in sixth grade, concerned himself with the extra minutes added to his commute. He would have to backtrack to get to work each morning. The commute to junior high meant longer distances between us.

One Saturday, we drove from our house to the junior high campus and then to his workplace. He timed the minutes as they changed on the console of his white Buick Riviera. I sat with my hands folded in my lap as he drove, fearful it would take too long, but certain that any other school was not really an option.

"Public school?" my father bellowed the one time I'd mentioned it. "They'd eat you alive." I tried to picture who or what would "eat me alive." I imagined beatings from bullies and other consequences of being one of the smart ones in class, images I got from after school specials on TV.

My father won out to some degree when he made me fear public school, but I won as well. The trip to Oakcrest Junior High added only ten extra minutes to his commute.

I enrolled in seventh grade at Oakcrest and was introduced to the petite principal who casually informed students that she moonlighted as an aerobics instructor. The campus was small, unadorned. The cement yards were surrounded by ivy-heavy fences that separated us from the apartments and houses surrounding the campus. A bungalow classroom sat like an afterthought amidst the cement courts. The main classrooms were on either side of a narrow courtyard. The main office was an A-frame house that reminded me of Snow White and the Seven Dwarfs. The one set of tiled bathrooms did double duty as locker rooms, complete with a dark inner chamber of group showers. The boys' and girls' bathrooms were separated by one heavy wall. Our voices echoed from one bathroom to the next with an eerie dungeon-like quality.

~

My first intrigue when I approached the campus teeming with students in this small cement space: male teachers. Second intrigue: older students, female, who looked like high school seniors and not the ninth graders that they were, strolling about wearing high-end, brand-name clothes, jewelry, and haughty expressions on heavily lipsticked and rouged faces.

Then, too, there were the negotiations for attention, popularity, and status that had been more submerged in elementary school. Junior high seemed to pulse with the need.

Something different pulsed in me, too. I began collecting little plastic cases that contained gray and black and heather-colored eye shadows. Tiny little brushes accompanied the squares of luminescent powder. I hid these, and the tube of white lipstick and black eyeliner pencil, in my book bag. When I left my father's car, my face had just one coat of foundation; by homeroom, I had a smooth line of black around my eyes and a heavy coat of metallic gray shadow on my eyelids. I learned my make-up routines from Veronica and Abigail.

On campus, my classmates and I could be found in Mr. Connell's homeroom: *We don't need no education!* and *Hey, Teacher, leave us kids alone!*, the Pink Floyd refrains we boomed in unison to Mr. Connell's delight. This act did not catch on with other teachers, so we kept it within the confines of homeroom. Our class traveled together from homeroom to math to art to biology to English on the tiny campus, the smallest school I would ever attend.

Between classes, we could be found lolling around the aluminum benches or tussling against the catering trucks. On rare rainy days, we were stuck inside the humid classrooms after school, waiting for annoyed parents who had fought traffic to retrieve us.

As my parents became more volatile, I became more oblivious to the dramas of my fellow students. I now had dramas of my own, all of which required secrecy and a fair share of acting. Everything at home was normal. Everything was fine. With Mr. Ivers in my life now, I felt strangely outside of things, but the new places I found inside myself were suddenly starting to feel unpredictable, explosive, alive.

NOVEMBER
1986

On Monday, after that first monumental phone call, I looked more closely at Mr. Ivers.

His hair was black, a true, jet black, with an occasional auburn strand in the midst of its soft, natural curl. He was jovial, always joking. His laugh commonly peppered his conversations, his classroom lectures. His hazel eyes, which sometimes cast a strong greenish glint, were small. His glasses resembled an aviator's, only with clear lenses. I wondered how old someone had to be in order to wear such unattractive, bland frames. The thought made me touch my own glasses, mottled brown, square frames, which I chose (to my mother's dismay) because they resembled the frames James Dean wore in the poster I taped to the wall of my bedroom. ("Those are men's frames!" she cried.)

Mr. Ivers had pale features that turned ruddy, a harsh blush I would later learn became more pronounced when he had a few beers, or a snort of cocaine, or when he was angry. Later, when he grew out his facial hair, it was predominantly red, and tickled my enamored imagination as well as parts of my skin. There was the distinct cleft in his chin, which I latched onto, recognizing it as a feature many women remarked upon in men. The gap in his top two front teeth was the clincher for me, and would later become one standard by which I found people distinctly attractive.

But I was not in love with Mr. Ivers's appearance.

At thirteen, I thought I was attracted to blondes with blue or green eyes. I assumed that my first crushes figured into the equation: first kiss with a boy was James Keller, a fast little runner boy who had a dirty blonde head of hair; first (prohibited, dangerous, electric) kiss with a girl was Abigail, friend since kindergarten, first language German, blonde, who kept her green eyes open the entire time.

I secretly eyed Mr. Ivers's ties, though his whole look was something I deemed too formal. I could do without the cardigan sweaters that reminded me of old men. The sweaters matched his shirts and slacks perfectly, and at school he was never without one, even on the hot days. His occasional light pink button-up shirts were a subject of ridicule behind his back—my classmates called the colors "so gay!" and I was too uncertain to challenge such a judgment.

Instead, I stared at the knot of his tie and then returned his gaze, wondering if he was able to discern my secret impulse to remove it.

Instead, this secret lingered, smoldering, until two years later when I got the courage to share it with him. Until then, I busied myself with scenes that had no endings in my fantasies: letting my thumb and forefinger run down the broad, silky length of the tie, slowly, feeling my fingertip on the other side, slowly undoing the knot. The image dissolved.

After school, as my classmates and I waited for parents to pick us up, his attire changed dramatically. My attraction ebbed when he reappeared wearing sweatpants, a wrinkled t-shirt, and a baseball cap. The saving grace was that I could let my eyes glance over the front of his sweats, wondering about the state of his penis, trying to imagine exactly what it looked like, then giving up because I had no other image to compare it to.

I was not my full height at thirteen, and Mr. Ivers, though not tall, seemed to tower satisfyingly next to me. His frame was stocky; his thick, pale skin sprouted black hairs. He exuded a masculine energy that framed me in a more feminine light, something I grappled with as my hips expanded, my breasts filled out. I wanted to stand beside him, or better yet, in front of him, just close enough to hook up with the energy flow, the unspoken promise of sex, with someone bigger, heavier, more solid than I felt myself to be.

NOTES ON AN EXCAVATION:

ANY GIVEN DAY

I open the *L.A. Times* website and on the first page of the *L.A. Now* blog, the headline "Married Teachers Guilty of Having Group Sex with Students" greets me. The headline will vary depending on the day, but they continue, an ongoing litany.

It is as simple as typing "teacher guilty" into a news outlet's search field. A stream of articles featuring teachers suspected or convicted of preying on their students appears. Often, they rise to the top, becoming *interesting* news, even as these stories become more common.

It is any given day.

Scandals rock the Los Angeles Unified School District. Sometimes the difference between this school year and last is that on their first day of a new school year, students are welcomed by more than just their teachers. Psychiatric social workers might be present, as well as school police and news vans.

There is a special language to learn when discussing these matters.

"Lewd conduct" is interchangeable with "lewd and lascivious conduct" which is interchangeable with "lewd acts." The word "lewd" seems to carry an incomprehensible weight in these phrases.

In my own circumstances, it would be years before I could find the words that would fit my experience.

I scan the news stories and waste little time on the photos, usually mug shots with a dark gray wall behind the subject. Sometimes, the subject is even smiling, or attempting to lift the corners of their mouths. There's really nothing I ever see that would make these subjects stand out if I saw them at an amusement park, a grocery store, or a classroom.

I did find myself intrigued by one recent news story, though. My mother thought to bring it up to me.

In this story, a male teacher leaves his family, resigns from his job, and shacks up with a former student. They maintain that they are in love, and that nothing untoward occurred until the student was a legal adult—eighteen years of age, the magic number. This becomes a national headline in March 2012. One month later, the now former teacher is arrested for having sexual relations with an entirely different student, who was seventeen years old. His eighteen-year-old girlfriend leaves him. A month later, she returns to him, even though he's out on bail and due back in court, charged with sex with a minor.

I have so much to say to these girls.

And then I have nothing to say.

I want to walk arm in arm with them, look them in the eyes, listen to them. And then I want to stand silent, still, away, observing their decisions, if you can call them that.

Nearing forty, a part of me just doesn't get it anymore.

Another part of me gets it. Like, *viscerally*.

It is any given day.

In one dark corner of my own history, I had fantasies fueled by my teacher, too.

These fantasies involved packing everything we owned and moving to Montana—his idea, since I had no concept of Montana. I had only been as far as Washington State. We were waiting for the magic number to fall into place, the numbers one and eight taking on ridiculous meanings all their own.

I learned later—years after I had turned eighteen—that my former teacher had misdeeds with other underage girls.

I open a website. I watch the news. I listen to the radio and hear another tragic display of power dynamics at their worst.

It is any given day.

NOVEMBER 1986

A week passed.

A week where my stomach felt light and empty whenever I stepped foot into English class. Two weeks. Three.

One night on the phone, Mr. Ivers asked me for a note from my parents that would sanction our phone calls.

My stomach contracted. I held the telephone receiver away from my mouth so he wouldn't hear my intake of breath.

"Okay," I said, scrambling to think of something to follow up with. I willed my voice to sound even. "But my mom already knows we talk on the phone, and that it has to do with school." The lie felt sticky and fell to pieces in my mouth, like gum chewed for hours.

"Just get me the note," he said, before turning the conversation back to basketball, teaching English, or the way my mouth made him weak with desire as he sat behind his desk every day.

When we hung up, I looked at the floor, deciding how to come up with a note.

There was no question: I would ask my mother and not my father for the note. I knew I could explain to my mom that this teacher was kind, and helpful, and loved my writing, and that there was absolutely nothing abnormal about talking to him on the phone. "He talks like we do," I said to her finally. "He knows how kids like me feel."

She wrote the note, eyeing me with her cloudy brown eyes. She went back to sipping her orange soda and vodka.

I tiptoed back to my bedroom, as I tiptoed throughout the house all the time.

I picked up the cream-colored Princess phone gingerly, as if it might break into a million pieces.

~

In the yellow legal pad, I wrote.

"Never, ever write anything down about us," Mr. Ivers had cooed into my ear. "You can't tell a soul. I don't care who you trust. I'm totally fucking-A serious."

I agreed, and turned the yellow legal pad over on the bed to avoid staring at the sheets of written-on paper.

I complained about my alleged best friend Abigail, about the boys at school, and about my parents and their unraveling. Their divorce was around the corner though the word itself was not yet spoken.

I felt justified in telling Veronica and Abigail about Mr. Ivers. They were the ones who meant the most to me, who I looked up to, the ones I wanted to know that I was in something dangerous and deep. I wanted to tell them particularly after Mr. Ivers went on and on about the girlfriend who left him. I had no such story to offer. I was a boyfriend-less thirteen-year-old, still wondering if touching myself every night and my past hobby of making out with girls in my bedroom closet would put me in hell.

I told these friends about the new development in my life, our teacher and I talking on the phone. Their eyes got big and their mouths fell open as I repeated the words, tallied the hours of phone calls. I swore them to secrecy, and their lips became tight with incredulous smiles, eyes shining with curiosity.

After telling my friends, I noticed something different in myself. It felt like a haze of dirt followed me wherever I went. I learned not to speak of my situation very often. My friends never spoke of it unless I brought it up, which was rare.

~

Mr. Ivers, or Jeff, as he began calling himself, made me aware of bodily responses, like the prickles of arousal that his scripted, well-detailed fantasies spoken aloud created in me.

In my own fantasies, I envisioned us at candlelight dinners in restaurants I conjured up in my head, a collage of restaurants I saw on soap operas and TV movies. I imagined our legs tangled underneath the table, the way the shadows and our silent waiter might lend danger and seduction to our meeting, as so often happened in movies: scenes of secrecy, pleasurable and monumental undoing.

He made his fantasies known to me and I listened, admiring his courage to share what I thought were secret places requiring special access. I learned to chuckle huskily and not directly answer questions like "Are your fingers inside of you?" or "Are you squeezing your tits like I would if I were there?"

My body stopped short of responding to the choreography he directed.

I listened instead, absorbed the words and sentiment, and played along. He provided erotic frameworks; I closed my eyes and focused on the tingle in my fingertips. My body was still mine, private, its workings hidden and mysterious even to me. I was vastly more comfortable daydreaming on my own, filling in empty scenes with abstract female bodies for pleasure and even more abstract male bodies to assuage my guilt.

I continued to document the formation of this new person I was becoming on the yellow pages, as though Mr. Ivers was helping to create me with his words and I was compelled to transcribe the transformation. As with all my journals, dating from the time I was six, I made sure to include the details of every admission he made, the ways I implored him for more attention without ever, I imagined, showing my true hand. I recorded the minutiae of our phone conversations and the encounters at school with an eye for the drama inherent in them, and also with an eye for what I was becoming.

He kept asking me if I ever wrote about us.

"Are you kidding?" I replied. "No. Of course not."

"Good. Because you can't. If I found out you did—"

I didn't want us to end, whatever the us was in the process of becoming.

DECEMBER 1986

That Christmas, I asked my mother for a copy of *Lolita*.

It arrived as all books given to me did: wrapped in Christmas paper, pages in the book revealing bills of various denominations—ones, fives, tens. *Surprise!*

It wasn't the money I was interested in, though.

It had a white cover. The title was spelled out broadly across the top. In the letters were the stratified sections of a picture of a young girl, smiling, wearing a hint of lip gloss.

My mother's writing in its opening pages:

My Baby,

> *Don't get any ideas.*
> *Love, Your Mom.*

She didn't ask why I wanted this book, didn't know that I heard the name "Nabokov" in a song by The Police, about a situation that sounded strangely similar to the one I was in.

~

After holiday break, I was trying to read *Lolita*, trying to follow all the words, but I was giving up on the French and getting exasperated with the English. I reread sections about Humbert's fascination with prepubescent girls and wondered at them, myself. My body, I decided, was not prepubescent, which accounted for people's eyes widening when I told them how old I was.

I sifted through the descriptions and decided Humbert Humbert was a sick man. I felt sorry for him as I turned each page carefully after several thick minutes of struggling to decipher this prose.

One afternoon, Eva and I were loitering in Mr. Ivers's classroom after school with a few other students. I decided to take a seat at a desk in front. Eva was blah-blahing about the homework assignment. Another kid stood in the doorway, bouncing a basketball, yelling to someone outside over his shoulder. I whipped out the book from my bag and pretended not to notice when Mr. Ivers strode across the classroom and chided the kid with the ball about taking it out onto the courts. When he was done, I stared intently at the book, and then up at him, then down at my book. My eyes were scanning the book, then the linoleum, checking to see if his loafers came into my line of sight, signaling his nearness. I read, then reread, a single paragraph.

I looked up and asked, "Mr. Ivers, what's 'folly' mean?"

I knew the answer but I wanted engagement, acknowledgment of some kind.

He sighed good-naturedly. He moved to the cabinet behind his desk. Out came an oversized dictionary.

"Oh, forget it." I rolled my eyes and pretended to return to this book with plenty of other words I didn't understand completely.

Eva was twittering someone's ear off nearby. There were at least four other kids in the room, in their own bubbles of conversation. My mom was coming to get me in about thirty minutes.

Mr. Ivers set down the dictionary on the desk in front of me. He poked my shoulder with a finger, which felt like a dare.

"Is this word from the nasty book you're reading?" he asked.

"It's not nasty, it's a classic," I sniffed, pushing my glasses up on my nose with one finger.

"It's about the young girl who wham-bams the older man, isn't it?" He smirked. I looked up at him like he was crazy, but my face betrayed me, softened into a quiet smile.

"What word is it, Wendy?" he asked, leaning over me to open the dictionary to "F."

I was having a hard time breathing regularly. I wanted him to know this. He was so close to me now, his cologne driving me a little mad, and there was that tickle in my lower belly and heat rushing to my crotch.

"Folly," I said, trying to appear calm. I listened to the outskirts of our conversation. Other kids in the class were talking, reading, doing homework. Nothing was askew. We were safe.

"Fondle?" he asked. "Fondle? You want to know what 'fondle' means?" He gently poked me in the shoulder again, chuckling. I could hear the purr in his voice, the one I was getting used to hearing on the phone almost every night. I could hardly take a full breath. If I did, I imagined I'd be taking in some of his breath along with mine, and there might be an explosion of flame.

"Whatever," I said loudly, pointedly. "Folly. Folly! I found it. Here, right here." I read the definition loudly enough for others to hear.

When I finished he slapped the large volume shut.

"Never be afraid to use the dictionary," he said, smiling mysteriously, and returned the book to the cabinet. I looked at the back of his sweater and my mouth felt wet, slack. I breathed in deeply, as if preparing to go underwater.

1987

1987

Hours upon hours of talking about record albums, song lyrics, then looking up words in the dictionary, feeling as though I constantly need to catch up with him intellectually, the age difference suddenly feeling like a chasm, until we get to the boiling point, the point where it all comes down to *I'm so hard for you, you are IT, the most exciting thing at school* and I'm in bed, muffling my voice under a pillow with the phone to my ear, hand in my underwear, talking quietly, assuring, chuckling with my new sexy voice and realizing the hold, the power I have over this person who moans and grunts and flicks his tongue at me through the phone like I have never experienced before. This is no *kid*, this is no *boy*, this is no finger fuck in the park, this is no rush of kisses in a dark movie theater. This is sex across wires. This is gut-wrenching first-time-ever oozing red love. This will be hot angry tears and hanging up the phone, later. This will be promises broken and fingers touching clandestinely in classrooms. But right now, this is power in the curve of my hip, the way I turn to face him, the mystery of my turtleneck sweater, power in the sound of my whisper, power in the arch of my back and pout of my lips. This is fire, air, drowning, gushing, purging. This is illegal.

HOME
1987

Vodka splashing in a tall plastic tumbler, over ice, covered in orange soda. Over the years the plastic of the tumbler got scratched, worn away from the acidity of its liquids.

Overturned bottles on the moss-green carpet, the lair underneath the sink where the bottles hid. The miracle of television, three in a house, covering over the silence or the sounds of rage.

The calendar of mortgage bills.

The magic in the wall of gold gilded mirrors. The magic in a fort built of blankets and tray tables, the nights the parents were in love and took to their bedroom.

The black wigs and rarely-used neckties in closets.

The king-sized bed for one, the hide-a-bed in another room that ruined my mother's back forever.

The backyard's dewy green lawn turned into a nest of brown pine needles and tumbleweed, the spiny thorned plants growing dangerous, the death of fruit trees.

The wayward ash from wildfires in the foothills. The pond scum, gutters bursting with packed-in dirt and leaves. The garage of shadow, webs, abandonment, oil on the concrete floor.

The decomposition of the patio, mushrooms growing in the carpet, records warped from sunlight and moisture when the ceilings fell away.

The wallpaper curling, smoke-darkened walls, fogged sliding-glass door.

Home.

EARLY
1987

In the 1980s, the Sherman Oaks Galleria, besides providing refuge for teenagers, also offered a variety of card and gift shops. I roamed their aisles reading sentiments embossed on the inside of pastel-washed greeting cards.

Cards with watercolor sunsets, lyrical words written in forest green or burgundy calligraphy; triple-folded cards with artwork on expensive paper; cards in the shape of seashells with glossy pink finish, or in the shape of hearts, purplish-red and desperate: I considered each one, picking up the card that spoke to me and would speak for me. I purchased almost one per week. I carried them home privately, in their slim white paper bags, closed my bedroom door, and chose a pink or purple ink pen. I opened my journal to serve as a hard surface, and composed the closest I could come to uninhibited love letters to Mr. Ivers.

Mostly, the cards were filled with questions. Are we really friends? Did he take me seriously? Should I be looking for a wedding card for him and his on-again, off-again girlfriend in the coming year? Did he really think I could write?

The things I felt like I couldn't say out loud I articulated with song lyrics: Blondie, ABBA, Echo and the Bunnymen, Bruce Springsteen, all of these and more were featured in capital letters, each line of the song separated by slash marks and cited by title, artist.

I imagined, years later, after he'd collected a trunk full, that they might be burned in an inferno of blue fire. Or that he might cut them up into little pieces and let them fly, so that each was a white paper insect, on a solitary journey far from his hands, his body.

I knew that he probably disposed of these letters, lyrics, and yearnings as soon as they had been read. They might disappear into trash cans, holes in the backyard. A match used to light up a bongload might also serve to burn my handwriting away into nothingness.

I, on the other hand, kept copies of some of the letters. Carbon paper suited my purposes. Some letters remained unsent, planting themselves in my journal.

I don't know why/I love you like I do/All the changes/You put me through...

He was smart in that way. Letters read, discarded. No evidence.

~

The classroom began to feel heavy with temptation, pleasure, disappointment, or ruin. The daily aftershocks of our clandestine relationship were shooting off the charts. The pendulum could swing violently one way, softly the opposite way, until I felt unraveled and wanting.

I was thrown into a rage of jealousy if Mr. Ivers spoke in class of his girlfriend, which he sometimes did. I might ignore his lecture, or leave class abruptly when the bell rang, instead of lingering. There were days when the small act of passing a piece of chalk from his hand to mine shook me to my core. In the midst of the classroom our fingers met, he tickled my palm quickly, grabbed at my fingers. There was a long, deep stare, a wetting of my lips in nervousness, a letting out of breath when I suddenly had the chalk in my grasp, my heart racing, wondering why I received it in the first place.

I attempted to quell the onslaught of heat that made my stomach light, legs weak.

I had the small cylinder of white chalk, and there was a class of students around me that carried on their own conversations and did not let on that they could see or feel the tide that threw me this way and that, or the erection Mr. Ivers had suffered, hidden by his pressed slacks.

I was scared for him.

I felt like he wasn't hiding us well enough, even as he expected me to keep my part of the secret. I knew the complexities of my classmates' teenage minds. The swell in the girls' blouses, the bulge in boys' pants, the hormones raging in a teenager's little finger, let alone body—anything was enough to set us off. Innuendos, crude and lascivious, thrashed about the classroom and the schoolyard. I suddenly felt left out of its wake, walking on air above such crassness.

I was submerged in a different ocean of innuendo. Mr. Ivers and I developed secretive looks and behaviors that quietly forced our attractions underground, but just below a malleable, ever-changing surface.

"Wear your black skirt tomorrow. No tights. Sit in the front row and casually uncross your legs. I'm dying to see what's underneath, Wendy. Just look up, look me in the eye and you'll see."

I wore my black skirt. I wore tights. I sat in the second row and prepared myself for his disappointment. I wondered what it might look like, this disappointment, as I made teeth marks on my ballpoint pen caps.

He was never disappointed. Instead, in the middle of lectures he punctuated with exclamations and rhetorical questions that made the class laugh with him, he looked directly at me. When the class carried on without him, laughter continuing, another snappy retort from Brian in the corner, a guffaw from Tony—through it all, Mr. Ivers held my gaze. Mere seconds passed, loaded with an energy I was becoming more familiar with, my eyes locked on his, my lips slightly parted, and his intense charge, the current that connected us from halfway across the room.

When he broke the gaze to reassert a friendly control over his classroom, he made sure to glance back every so often. I drank up the last bits of attention and refocused on my desk, my papers. My gaze shifted to Abigail, who sketched in the corner of her pages, or Veronica, who was hunched over her desk, chin in hand. I tried to gauge their awareness, wondering if anyone caught the current midway, checking for any curious looks at me or at the teacher.

None.

Mr. Ivers continued his informal lecture on commercials and propaganda, and introduced our next project, to create a commercial to perform in front of the class. What this has to do with English, I did not know. But I liked the idea. He seemed a smart man. Everyone liked him.

I smiled to myself and went back to writing on the naked pages in front of me.

MARCH
1987

Spring.

Field trips whisked us away from the stuffy classrooms into the world at large, the world I was becoming more independent in. The teachers accompanied us. My classmates and their small talk and pranks left me feeling saddled by their awkwardness but nevertheless eager to be outside.

One field trip took us to a play and after, to the Santa Monica Pier. The day felt hopeful, as though it would provide some semblance of adulthood, the freedom outside of a classroom, walking in the world with only a few adults per several students.

I found myself sitting next to Mr. Ivers at the play, which irreparably erased any image or impression I might have had of the play, including the name or the content or the venue. The most memorable moment in that pocket of time when the lights were out, actors moving upon a stage, my hands stationed in my lap: his voice, as he leaned over to whisper softly, "I feel like slipping under your skirt." His cologne lingered near my face, an invisible veil that made me swoon.

After the play, our class traipsed down the pier.

"Well, we made it to the beach," he said to me. I flashed on the conversations, too numerous to count, that featured fantasies of meeting at the beach, spending a day, or even a few hours staring at the ocean together, picking up shells, just talking without having to punch buttons or hold pieces of plastic to our ears.

"Hmm," I answered. "This isn't good enough."

I wanted the empty beaches up the Pacific Coast Highway; we were at the pier with its arcades, hot dog smells, and shops that sold postcards of thin, blonde, tan women in bikinis. There were too many people around us, and they reminded me, painfully, of our true identities, even as I wished them away so that it was just us, only us.

"You're right, it's not good enough," he agreed. "You wore your damn leggings."

He gave me a wink before moving into the throng of students, unreachable. He became my teacher again.

~

On the phone, the night before this class excursion, he'd created aloud a scene of him giving me a ride home after the field trip. I giggled at this fantasy and wondered if any piece of it, even just a shard, could come true.

What happened was this: after the field trip, me, Tammy, and Mary took the bus to Jerry's Deli. Mr. Ivers was due to meet us at the bowling alley, an event that both Tammy & Mary's parents had sanctioned. I knew I could say anything about my afterschool wanderings to my mother and she would believe me.

After we ate, Mr. Ivers met us at the adjoining bowling alley. I made some excuse to remove my leggings in the women's restroom, my legs naked under my wool shorts. No one seemed to notice.

Tammy dominated the conversation. I watched her friendly rapport with Mr. Ivers. Mary seemed more inert, needful of being pulled into the joke or conversation, a bit wary of all the silliness. I remained my observant self, though I involuntarily felt myself laughing deeply and often, thanks to Tammy's presence. I felt thirteen, which was becoming more rare. *We are bowling*, I thought. *This is safe. I'm having fun.*

Tammy's mom arrived to pick up Mary and Tammy after two games. They both lived close to the bowling alley, south of Ventura. I felt my mouth readying to announce that I'd be riding the bus home. *It's okay, I don't need a ride*, I rehearsed silently.

"Oh, I can give you a ride. It's not a problem," Mr. Ivers said in front of the girls as they got into Tammy's mother's car.

I glanced in their direction, the girls who were getting safe passage home. They didn't seem aware of the innuendo that had flown around the four of us in the last two hours, the times he had leaned over to whisper in my ear. Maybe they accepted it as part of Mr. Ivers's demeanor. To me, he seemed a little too daring, combustible. I worked hard to disown these little comments, pretending I couldn't hear him. I flashed him looks that said *Quit it! They might hear you!*

But they were gone, and I was walking with him to his old green Porsche.

"So, down Laurel Canyon?" he asked, opening the door for me.

"All the way down," I said, folding myself into the small, low seat.

"I like the sound of that," he growled, and started the car. His aging Porsche made a loud chugging sound that reminded me of the cars on tracks at Disneyland.

"Hey, you don't think they got what was going on, do you? I mean, c'mon, I don't think they'd know sexy if it bit 'em in the ass." I paused. I really wasn't sure, but knew I had to maintain that no one knew anything.

"I don't know. We don't really talk about stuff like that," I answered, looking out at the other cars in the lot. Mercedes, Ferrari, BMW. A lone station wagon. Vanity plates.

"Yeah, why would you?" Mr. Ivers asked me. "You're light years ahead of 'em!" He pulled out of the parking lot. "Wanna ride, little girl?" he joked as we turned on to Laurel Canyon.

Alone with me, he suddenly couldn't stop talking.

"God, seeing you lean down, with your ass just right, releasing the ball—in a fucking bowling alley, I can't believe it. I was getting so hard!"

"You were?" I turned to look at him with fear and fascination.

"Yeah! Didn't you notice? I couldn't stand up. I had to stay in that fucking chair with the little desk on it or it would've been over—totally obvious." He put one cupped hand over his mouth and bellowed into the air, "Ladies and gentleman, the man on lane five must leave the premises immediately, no hard-ons allowed in the bowling alley!" He laughed. I smiled and stared straight ahead.

"You really have no idea what you do to me, do you?" he asked after some silence.

I didn't reply. There was something important about never fully acknowledging what was happening between us. It was the thinnest bubble, a membrane I might burst if I settled on it for too long. I wished for more and more miles between his barreling green Porsche and my house.

"You know, Wendy, I'm hard now."

With one hand on the wheel, he used the other to lift the cuff of my shorts so it rode the top of my thigh.

"Why don't you just pull those shorts up a little, just enough so I can see a little more..."

He uttered a low moan and looked at the road, his hand on my leg, warm. I pressed my back into the seat, goosebumps lacing my arms, and I felt myself shifting in my seat.

At Burbank Boulevard he said, "Here, feel this," and took my hand. He placed it on his crotch and I felt a large, firm *something* underneath the jeans he changed into for this afterschool activity.

This was the crucial moment. It always came to this. In the three or four instances when I had occasion to make out with boys, this is where it always culminated, my hand led to this spot, where it felt like a secret nesting animal pulsing underneath jeans, khakis, cotton.

I did the only thing I know how to do. My hand lightly pressed, cupped the hardness, rubbed my palm and fingers over it. I wondered if he liked it and tried to remember that I had done this before, just not with him. I shot looks at cars nearby as we continued towards Roscoe Boulevard, closer and closer to my house. I lost track of his litany of suggestions ("Ooh, yeah, right there,") and compliments ("How can you make me feel this way?"). I tried to appear a normal girl staring ahead in the passenger seat of a green Porsche, one hand in my lap, the other on him. I let his free hand caress my thigh, inches from the crotch of my panties.

Finally, we neared my neighborhood.

"Can you just drop me off at the gas station up there?" I heard myself say.

"Of course. Yes." He pulled into the station. Our hands found their appropriate places: I secured my book bag to my shoulder, he traced one finger around my knee and returned his hand to the wheel. The car chugged loudly in idle.

"Okay, see you later. Thanks for letting me give you a ride home," he called out over the car motor as I slammed the door. I smiled, waved, started walking.

It was hard to say goodbye to this man for whom I was losing an identifier. He was no longer "Mr. Ivers." His first name did not slide off my tongue as it did in my fantasies. There was the now-familiar empty space, a space where, as we parted, I inserted the language silently, the sentiment I believed I was living for, even if only in my imagination.

Smile, wave.

The green car slid back into traffic.

Bye, I mouthed. *I love you*, I said to the sidewalk.

APRIL
1987

"You know that this is not just all about lust."

"Sure," I said. "I know."

It was eleven at night, our usual hour for talking that sometimes stretched into early morning.

"Because sometimes, I find myself wondering things…"

"Like?" I offered. I was hunkered down between the sheets and blankets of my bed, facing the wall, letting the phone touch my mouth, my chin, as I whispered into the receiver.

"Like, what it would be like if we got married, down the line. I mean, it's not so far-fetched."

I squeezed my eyes shut and prayed he would say it again so I would know this was real. This can't be. Married? Is he reading my mind? A tentative hand slipped over the front of my underwear. One ear stayed above the covers, tuned for noises outside my door.

"You're amazing, and I just want to keep knowing you. I know you're just gonna get more and more intense with every year, and I can hardly wait. It's fucking torture. It's a bad joke."

I laughed softly with him, willing myself to sound as rueful as he did.

"Well, Mr. Ivers, you should know that when I'm twenty-three, I'm going to be big-time," I announced in response.

"What is this Mr. Ivers crap?" he asked. He sounded hurt yet amused. "Quit it. Call me Jeff. Can you do that?"

"Whatever," I answered, blowing off this suggestion. It just felt too weird on my tongue. "Don't you get the feeling, though, that there'll be lots of people from my class who'll make it big?" I paused to see if he was with me. "Like, maybe when I'm twenty-three," I heard him sigh wistfully when I said the magic number, "I might open up the newspaper, and there'll be Brian on the front page. Doing something amazing. Famous."

"Yeah," he purred, "and then you'll fold up the paper and say 'Fuck me, Jeff.'"

"It's not all about lust, huh?" I chuckled in the new husky voice I achieved after hours of talking with him. I turned underneath the covers to face the other side of the room, switching the cream-colored receiver to my other ear.

"Lust isn't what makes me want to call you as soon as I get home every day," he said.

And I believed him. He told me it would be an awesome summer, so much would change, and that he'd show me exactly how he felt about me. I didn't mention to him that I had my doubts, especially with regard to where his girlfriend would fit into the picture he drew for me. She occasionally appeared from seemingly nowhere to wrench him from everyday life and then drop him back in, angered and hurt. I wondered how much she would figure into "our" summer. I wondered if I could hook up with someone else that would get my mind off this man. The women in my fantasies became hazier, and in fact, were often contorting themselves into fantasies Mr. Ivers had illustrated for me.

And we kept right on talking into the night, as he lay into me about education, college, success. I wandered in and out of the conversation, dozing, dreaming until it was time to hang up the receiver and sleep.

And it seemed true that it was not *all* about lust.

I listened with rapt attention as he detailed problems. Issues with family, expectations he couldn't seem to meet, the fucked-up relationship with the sometime/long-term girlfriend, and how he had a hard time talking to his friends about his personal problems.

As soon as he said this, I stepped up to plate.

I told him about my parents, their alcoholism. He told me about his father, whom he described as a recovering alcoholic. I practically glowed with recognition, this coincidental parallel between us.

I got a short, heartfelt lecture about how alcoholism was hereditary and that he hoped I'd take care of myself.

"Why?" I asked. I wanted to hear what I meant to him and I wanted to hear it *now.*

"Because I *care.*" He paused. "Because I consider you a good friend. And maybe because there might be a future for us."

No adults except Mr. Ivers were privy to my crumbling relationship with my parents, whose own lives were falling like dirt through open hands.

I spent more time crying into a pillow than talking or thinking about my parents, their ongoing fights or silence, my father's gradual disappearance from our lives.

I had decided that if my parents divorced, I must stay with my mother. I felt she needed me more than my father did. I was intent on staying at the same school as my friends, and my father would not be around to ask why the phone was ringing at all hours.

After learning that Mr. Ivers and I shared a common experience, I opened my journal to relate this revelation. I could tell him anything, and he, me.

Heaven, I wrote on the page. *It feels like this.*

MAY
1987

The written inscription read: *To Wendy, Big 14!*

The book was hardbound, sans dust jacket, with a sepia-toned cover and black binding. In a simple cursive, *A Treasury of Khalil Gibran* was embossed on the spine between two short, flowered scrolls. The writing and the scrolls were a dull gold color, lending the book an air of age and beauty I was not used to possessing.

I recognized that in his ballpoint pen scrawl, Mr. Ivers was attempting to maintain a friendly distance from me.

Read and enjoy! he wrote. *This book was meant to be read and reread as you get older and wiser in the ways of the world.* He used stale phrases like "passage of time" and "living of life," words that I saw as condescending to my fourteen-year-old mindset, words spoken from adult to child.

I quickly forgave him upon reading the next sentence.

You have the ability to write like this—someday I hope you reach that point, the "you" underlined, the sentence open-ended, lacking a period to stabilize its sentiment.

There was no missive of love, no cordial regards or sincere closing; only *Happy B-day*, and below that, *Mr. Ivers 1987.*

1987

Sometimes I stood naked on the closed toilet seat in my mother's bathroom. In the mirror over the sink I could see my body from my nose down to my calves. The shower blasted nearby, awaiting my entrance.

A tentative hand slipped like a curtain over one of my breasts. I watched the flesh quiver slightly and my knees trembled. I put one hand out and steadied it on the window frame next to me. The blinds were shut like so many eyelids. The door was locked so that I was alone with the mirror.

I put one finger to my mouth and traced my lips slowly.

I watched this body in the mirror: the flat, naked stomach, the brown shoulders, my pubic hair that seemed strange and messy on the landscape of smooth skin.

I looked down at the puffy toilet seat cover, gauging its ability to hold my weight. I turned so that I could see the curve of my butt. Something about looking at my body this way made me feel like there was a dam breaking inside me, slowly but surely.

I saw something sexy, something I wanted, and yet it was here, it was my own.

Behind many veils, shadows I carefully placed in my memory, I replayed briefly, almost wistfully, how I used to lie underneath

Abigail on her bed, playing the girlfriend to her rendition of boyfriend, the door closed, our breathing noisy and excited as we kissed passionately. Fear crept around the memory, squelching it, and I absently switched my thoughts to those of the magazine articles littering my bedroom. I stared hard at the shapes in the mirror. I compared the size of my breasts to my butt. I wished my boobs would transform into C-worthy cups. I turned so I was looking at my profile and stuck my butt out to examine it. My hand outlined its smooth shape, the muscle underneath, the curve from lower back to fleshy mound, to the hidden place underneath, where the skin was soft and indented. I let out a breath and knew, instantly, the kind of desire I might inflict on someone else, and the way I wanted to inflict it, like a masterful chess move. The knowledge slipped away just as suddenly, as my eyes examined a slight dimpling in the flesh, the dreaded foreshadowing of something that right then I wanted no part of.

My mother's heavy steps sounded on the kitchen floor. I hurriedly stepped down from the toilet and moved to open the shower door. When I turned back I saw my face full in the mirror amid the steam. I leaned close and puckered my lips once, then relaxed. I tried a smile I wanted to test on Jeff, something for the classroom, something that could hold all that I wanted to be, what I thought he wanted me to be. I saw my expression go from fourteen to ageless, my mouth parted slightly, looking strangely sexual and yet silly, the look reserved for demure Playboy bunnies that I had glanced at, quick as a flash, in magazine racks.

A moment later I recognized myself again. I stared into my own eyes for a moment and turned, stepping into the shower and closing the door solidly behind me, letting the steam engulf me.

JUNE
1987

Shake it, shake it, bay-beh, the synthesizer-enhanced voice of David Bowie crooned over and over.

The volume was turned up high, unusual for me, the girl who frequently turned down the volume on her mother's stereo. I chalked up her loud listening behavior to lack of consideration and immaturity, and the fact that my father was inexplicably away from home for longer periods of time, and therefore no longer around to complain.

On this June day, I replaced the needle on the 45 for the third time, sang along, and flopped down on my bed to replay Mr. Ivers's—Jeff's—first visit. From my bed, I glanced around the room, contemplating which images from my bedroom he took home with him, pondered over, discarded.

After approaching every room as if my mother might be hiding in one (and hearing constant reassurances from me that she was safely at work, a half-hour's drive away), he entered my bedroom.

He remarked on my collection of James Dean postcards, photos, and the black and white poster next to the television set that featured a smiling, cocky Dean. My fiber optic flower lamp had been plugged in absently, a feature of my room that he chuckled at, pointing out,

"Ah, yes, interesting. Goes good with smoking out, eh?" I guessed he must mean marijuana, but I was still sort of inexperienced with it. I nodded like I knew what he meant.

Photographs of the eighth grade camping trip with my homeroom were displayed next to my bed so I could see them as I drifted off to sleep. The photos had a golden hue to them from the angle I chose. There were the faces of Veronica, Abigail, me. Veronica and her dyed black hair, her sleeveless mock turtleneck and silver chains and necklaces. Abigail, who I was disliking on an alternate-day basis, peered out from underneath bleached white hair, the strands of her bangs crispy with the black mascara she used to create dramatic streaks.

I looked at her face in the photo and felt a frown form on my lips. I stubbornly suffered through Abigail's fits of rage and deep sorrow as she negotiated her first relationships with boys and overused the word "love." Her attentions to me shortened, became more pointed, and I was feeling the distinct sense that I was someone she felt she could take advantage of, and that this was something we both knew but didn't talk about. We also didn't talk about our own diverted attentions toward Veronica. I pondered this realization as my finger touched the gloss of the picture. A hazy thumbprint appeared over Abigail's face.

Mr. Ivers leaned over my unmade bed, scanned the photos, hmmming and pointing, "Hah! There's Veronica. Oh look, Brian's mid-prank in this one!" I barely registered his comments. He kept moving around the room, investigating with long glances everything adorning my walls. My blood felt like it was pushing a fast path through me.

I abruptly abandoned my replay of the afternoon and got up to change the record to one I cherished as a mere twelve-year-old, a radio hit by the British band Human League. I threw myself back down on the bed, the springs recoiling against my back. I sang along in a mock British accent, Here comes the mirror man! The clock's digital face told me that there were still hours to go before my mother would be home from work.

My eyes darted around the room, looking for other tiny remnants he might have honed in on while he was here. He hadn't stayed long, didn't linger, just enough time for a well-planned tease of tongue and touch.

I believed Jeff and I were friends. I wanted to be content with this much. I thought of his new mantra, his insistence that love never enter the picture, at least not the kind you fell into. I let out a sigh and waited for the needle to pick itself up. The record revolved dumbly on the stereo.

The night before on the phone we had mapped out this first visit, certain my mother and father would be at work, no danger. Then he changed the subject.

"Wendy, you need to promise me that you'll pursue writing."

"Yep," I answered.

I enjoyed the reaction I got from him, the urging, the near-pleading, when I acted blasé, uninterested, supremely casual as he spoke of my future.

"Journalism, magazines, something. You could be a lyricist, anything. I just hope you follow through." I hear him take a drink and swallow. "I want you to give me back that paragraph you wrote, the one I assigned. I'm going up to my mom's next weekend and I want to show it around so they can see what kind of talented kid I'm dealing with."

"Uh, okay," I answered. I switched the phone to my other ear, which felt equally hot and uncomfortable. "I just have to look for it. I think I threw it away."

Would he ask me again? Did he really want to show it off? It all sounded so weird to me, so unnatural, this extreme interest and praise.

I was still writing my book, which was becoming harder to keep in one binder. And the notebook I had to write for his class had become more about sharing my thoughts and feelings with him than anything else.

"You just have this thing," he continued. "Unlimited potential." He rambled on and I tuned out, his language a mixture of melodramatics, earnest coaching, and fortune-telling guidance. "I'll put you through college if I have to," he said.

I listened. I couldn't take this seriously. Of course I'd go to college, but right now I wanted to be left alone with my Stephen King books. I wanted to read Khalil Gibran when I feel inspired to, but I wanted to read the words slowly, savoring them, continuing my underlining of beautiful images and profound insights I didn't completely understand.

Still, I hung onto the words. Unlimited potential. The words reminded me of things spoken in the midst of familiar, fertile dreams.

I thought about his words and rearranged myself on the bed, scooting myself down and onto my side, my hands meeting underneath my ear in a prayer-like pose. My knees pressed against my chest. It felt far more satisfying to consider the tangible elements of the past day. I lifted myself on an elbow and let the fingers on one hand trace the areas beneath my breasts, where a small field of hickeys hid like violets under my t-shirt. I thought of the butterfly of his tongue landing on my stomach, my hips, in a feathery, fickle manner that made me squirm. I allowed the reliving of the day to take place yet again, the colorful re-imagining in my head to rewind, play, rewind, play. It was a scene I lost myself in, that could overpower the other words he said that I wanted to forget.

"Don't fall in love with me, Wendy. I fear that. So don't do it. Because it just wouldn't work out."

My stray hand found my hip. I wondered what happened to his fantasies of marriage down the road. Would it be a marriage without love? Did he know something about this kind of existence? Why would anyone want that kind of existence?

Love, love, love. I can *think* it. I just won't *say* it, I thought. I could make him believe anything.

I drifted off to sleep until the sound of my mother slamming the screen door woke me, pushed me back into the world of teenage girls who weren't in love, who couldn't be in love with their English teachers.

JULY
1987

A song by U2 became that summer's anthem. It played constantly on the radio, the signature electric guitar ringing out in my mother's car as we drove to the grocery store. It cried out from other people's cars, and on the boardwalk of Venice Beach. No matter which way you turned the dial, it was playing somewhere in the summer of 1987.

"So, have you found what you're looking for?" Jeff asked me. We were listening to the same radio station, and I heard the electronic echo as the song played over our phone line.

"No." I looked down at my bed, its sunny, flowery fitted sheet, unchanged for more than two weeks now. "Not quite." I wiggled my toes, awaiting his response, hoping I hit a nerve.

There was a pause, and a noise that sounded like it was coming directly from Jeff's throat.

"It seems like the women in my life are always saying that," he finally said with a self-deprecating chuckle.

I sighed and pressed my lips together. I was developing an intimate relationship with the act of lying. I wrestled with this new association silently, in between the sentences in our every conversation.

On another night, we got disconnected, and I tried calling him for the next half-hour. All I got was a busy signal. I punched the numbers again and again, getting more confused and annoyed by the second. I called the operator. She told me that his line was "in use." I told myself he'd merely unplugged his phone, not questioning why he'd do that in the middle of a conversation with me.

An hour passed and my phone rang, sounding shrill and angry. Jeff. He laughed, sounding high as a kite.

"So, my phone just shut down for a while there," he said between cackles. "And when I plugged it back in, it rang, and I figured it was you all pissed off at me thinking I hung up on you. I said, 'Well, now, I thought you might be calling me back,' and it's fucking Fara, man."

I continued listening, feeling an urge to slam the phone down, to punish both him and his girlfriend, who had just appeared again, out of nowhere, in the middle of our phone conversation.

"So, she says," his voice turned high-pitched and squeaky, "'Is Jeff there?' and I said, 'Oh, yeah, it's me! I thought you were someone else!'" He paused again to cackle and take a swig of, no doubt, a beer. "And then she says, 'Were you talking to some little bitch? Your line's been busy for a whole hour and you weren't home last night!'"

My breath caught when I heard he wasn't home the night before.

"So I just told her I was talking to my dad and my phone got fucked up somehow," he finished, his voice getting smaller and slightly strained as he pulled away from the phone to reach for something. He returned to the mouthpiece, his voice suddenly loud and important. "I'm gonna call her back now. I just wanted to let you know what was up. I'll call you tomorrow, okay?"

I murmured assent. He hung up. I had been silent the entire time. He seemed not to have noticed.

~

It was startling to not see Jeff most days of the week like I had when school was in session. I knew we would see each other before long, at my classmate Tony's confirmation party. I knew this party had something to do with religion, but I neglected to inquire further.

Jeff was on Tony's A-list. Tony's parents loved Jeff, his ability to coach a winning junior high basketball team, his infectious humor.

My mother dropped me off at the low-lit, cavernous Italian restaurant.

I walked in and my eyes fell on Jeff, already throwing back Coronas with a big grin on his face. Properly attired in teacher-wear, he had a gray cardigan draped over a chair and his tie loosened just to the point of being noticeable. Our eyes met and a sexual thunder crested over the room that no one else seemed to feel but me.

This late afternoon event had been marked semi-formal. I had to sort this out for myself, not having been invited to much that required anything formal or semi-formal. The mid-length, form-fitting dress I wore felt like a costume. In fact, I felt strange being around Jeff and kids I'd mostly grown up with, wearing this weird dress. Jeff was loose, gripping cold bottles of beer, one after the other, his tie ever closer to coming completely undone.

When the other fourteen-year-olds tried to cajole each other into slow dancing, Jeff immediately arrived at my side, asked me, insisted, insisted more urgently, until I gave in and our fingers met. He situated one hand on my lower back and the other in my hand. Sickly sweet sentimental tendrils reached out and attached themselves to my heart as the sounds of the song "Stand By Me" played over the low-budget speakers. Tony's dad moved around the room with a bulky video camera, capturing images of Renee and Sheila giggling and pointing at the other kids dancing, heavy-metal Laura sulking in the corner, and me and Jeff slow-dancing. Jeff's breath smelled of beer as he whispered, "I have something to tell you. Later."

Nervous, I tried not to look any of my classmates in the face. I jumped when Jeff suddenly called out "Joe!" over my shoulder. "Get a shot of us!" I turned my face into his shoulder, feeling my pantyhose clinging to my legs unnaturally, the ringing in my ears, fear shaking its wings in my heart.

Jeff turned to the video camera as Tony's father lingered on us. In a booming voice he said to the lens, "C'mon, Wendy, show the camera how much you love Mr. Ivers!" I kept my eyes on my feet and hid a smile as we moved slowly among the swaying adults and teenagers.

"You look so hot in that dress," he cooed at me when the camera and Tony's father fell away into the darkness. "You know, dancing can be kinda like having sex with your clothes on." He pressed me closer and I tried to peer nonchalantly over his shoulder to see who, if anyone, was looking at us.

The song ended and a faster one started up. I moved away from him, realizing I was backing away, trying to smile. His inhibitions were clearly gone. He seemed miles away as he danced hypnotically to the beat.

I couldn't eat by the time dinner was served. Jeff stationed himself near me at all times, as I attempted conversation with my classmates about the advent of high school, the newness of having to buy a uniform for the Catholic school most of us would be attending in August.

"Wanna have sex?" Jeff stage-whispered from behind me as I talked to Renee in a corner. I turned and he was gone. Renee's face looked pinched and we laughed nervously. Shit. She heard. I steered the conversation to her, asked what classes she would take in high school, how she felt about the uniforms we had to buy at the store across the Valley.

"I gotta leave early. Got tickets to see the Dodgers," Jeff said by way of farewell as evening set in.

"Okay," I said. I sighed and wondered what time it was and when my mom might pick me up. I wanted to hold onto the curious thrill of his body near mine and the empty wake he left when he notified me of his departure. I left the banquet room and followed the signs to the restrooms.

Jeff appeared at the door of the women's bathroom before I could open it.

"Oh my god. I can't believe this."

"Believe it," he said, and then, "Check it out. Make sure no one's inside."

I peeked in, glanced at the one stall. Its door was wide open. I looked back at him and nodded. He gave a dramatic look-see of the immediate area. No one was nearby. We charged inside and he locked the bathroom door.

Gripped tight against each other, my back touching the cold tiled wall, his tongue found mine and the taste of beer hit me, the smell of his cologne tickling my nose. His hands traveled swiftly, urgently cupping one breast. His palms found the hard, icy wall. I arched my back so that I was pressed against him, timidly testing to see if he was hard.

"I love you."

We kissed again, and I closed my eyes. He pulled away.

"I love you," he repeated. I heard the tone of surprise. I stood there, letting my back relax into the tiled wall, imagining little cartoonish birds and stars flying around my head, whistling stupidly.

"Tell me who you love," he said, his hazel eyes inches from my brown ones.

Silence. I held my breath and listened for footsteps, my mind wildly calculating how we could leave this place unnoticed, wondering if he was really going to take off with the friend he brought and seemed to ignore and just go to the baseball game like nothing momentous had occurred. Frustration began to boil in my belly, rippling out into my arms.

"C'mon, Wendy." He dropped his head. I looked at his mussed black hair. I wanted to kiss him, touch his head, press my body to his again. "Tell me who you love," he said to the floor, then raised his head to search my face. My throat seized and I blinked back surprised tears.

He stared at me a moment. "Okay, tell me who you *like.*"

"You," I murmured, looking down at my white low-heeled shoes. One ankle was twisted, the smudge on the inside right shoe glaring at me. He lifted my chin with a finger and his mouth was on mine again.

He pulled away.

"I hate wanting you so bad," he said to the sink, and I was introduced to the uses of "love" and "hate" in the same scene, one in which I was a featured player. I was painfully aware of the clothes, the ridiculous dress, his suit, how artificial and clumsy the fabric felt against my skin.

"I'll call you tonight for sure, but it'll be some time around one a.m.," he said, touching my hand. He unlocked the door, peered out, gave me a wicked smile and stole away.

I stayed in the bathroom a minute more. I turned on the faucet and let the cold water splash against my palms.

I forced myself to rejoin the festivities in the banquet room. My mother picked me up soon after and drove me home, inquiring about who was at the party, if everyone was going to the same school the following month. I answered, feeling as if my mouth was full of words in another language. The phone didn't ring once that night.

I found out days later that the friend Jeff brought to the party and ignored had asked who I was.

"He asked me, 'Who was that girl in the blue and white dress?'"

I quickly switched the phone receiver to my other ear so I wouldn't miss his answer.

"So I told him: 'That's the girl I'm going to marry when she turns 18.'"

I heard him spit out the shells of sunflower seeds and pop some more into his mouth. He laughed. I swallowed and tried to laugh, wanting to believe, loving his voice, hating the possibility of untruth. Then I changed the subject.

≈

2:30 p.m. Days later. My house was wavy with heat. I wore gray wool shorts and a cotton eyelet blouse.

I was experimenting with clothes. The turtlenecks couldn't be touched in the swelter of summer. They hung in my closet forlornly like dark shells. The shorts felt a little scratchy on my thighs and my legs felt prickly from the shaving I had just given them in the shower. The radio was tuned to a classic rock station, and a band Jeff told me about, the Moody Blues, was playing. I half-listened to the words. My mom wouldn't be home until four, or later. Thank god, I thought, Maybe there'll be some traffic. Maybe she'll stop to get a pint of Popov.

I was barefoot and had all the lights turned out because it was so fucking hot I couldn't bear electricity. I trotted from my bedroom, yellow-tinted with the blinds open and sun touching the room, to the dark cave of the living room. I flitted from room to room, peeking out my bedroom blinds, moving the front door just a tad this way so I could see out the screen door, which was locked, but could easily be broken and entered.

My hair was longer than it was during the school year. It was just to my shoulders. I had played with Sun-In, but resolved to apply more drastic measures soon, like full-on bleach.

I heard a car pull up.

It was Jeff.

I pretended not to notice until he was practically at the screen looking in at me.

"What's up?" he asked with a knowing smile, and I allowed him in. I shut the door behind him. I wanted him to feel at home, to recall the last time he was here with fondness, to stay awhile.

2:45. We were moving from room to room. This time he made fun of the clutter surrounding the bed of my childhood. I wondered silently if we would be using this bed for anything today. I hated its springs that felt unpredictable, sharp. He nodded, assessing what was mine, as if comparing it to the last time he was here just weeks before, searching for miniscule changes. His eyes hit the yellow carpet, the small areas on the wall where I'd handwritten in markers my own poetry, plus lyrics I heard on 106.7 K-R-O-Q, Rock of the 80's! Then he turned around and started leading us back to the living room.

I was kicking myself now. *Why the hell would a twenty-eight-year-old man want to hang out in a fourteen-year-old's bedroom, anyway?* I tried to leave the disappointment behind in the abandoned bedroom, the ungranted wish that he would want to sit down, admire my things again, touch each one and connect it to me. Instead, I was following him down the hallway, feeling a gap open between us.

We were back in the cool of the living room. The swamp cooler whirred above our voices. The olive green carpet lent itself to the darkness, as did the couches.

But then there were the mirrors.

The wall behind the television was covered in mirrors. Each square of mirror glass was splattered with gold designs that I sometimes saw faces in. "Groovy mirrors," he remarked sarcastically. He ran a streaming commentary the entire time, but I only heard certain parts. I was nervous, expectant. I could tell he was trying to get a feel for the place, the people who populated it, who raised me. He was scanning the mirrors, the dark carpet, the enormous couches in a way that felt different than last time, like he was absorbing something I couldn't see. I inserted remarks into his commentary and we played off each other. I loved hearing him laugh. We were making silly conversation and I relished it, unsure what could happen next.

When he moved closer to me my skin felt as though it was opening up to drink in the air. He had already squeezed my ass, ran a hand down my torso and along my hip, somewhere between my bedroom and the return to the living room. It happened so fast, he even retracted his hand quickly, like he had burned himself, but recovered to act cool about it. I knew this was difficult. I tried to disown my own nervousness. I inched closer to him to let him know that his touch was okay with me, that in fact, it was what I wanted.

Chatting nervously, I jumped off the couch to check the kitchen clock. "It's three," I announced. "My mom will be home around four, but she usually stops at the market."

"I see," he said, and moved closer still, and suddenly, before I could think about what was happening, I was pressed against the sofa, and he was on the floor on his knees in front of me, swiftly pulling my scratchy wool shorts down my hips. Even at this moment, between him nuzzling the arch of my foot as it rode the air, running his lips over my calves, he was giving me a running commentary.

I heard that he wanted me so much, that he could hardly wait until school was over so he could get my clothes off and see what he'd been missing. I heard that I was sexy, soooo intense-looking, and that my panties were hot, and maybe I needed some help getting out of them. I was ecstatically pliant, pointing my toes, flexing my calf muscles, arranging my legs just so as he took me by surprise, his five o'clock shadow brushing my thighs, his hands alternately holding my one leg splayed out and the other pushing my panties to one side.

My head was thrown back, pressing into the soft flesh of the couch. I had never done any such thing on this couch—*I have never done any such thing*, I thought to myself. He was licking, murmuring, and I was responding, like a conversation, sigh with sigh, grunt with squeal, his tongue lapping and murmurs of what I hoped was satisfaction. Then his face was in front of me and he was undoing his belt. He looked like he was in a trance. I became witness to his penis, *my teacher's you-know-what!* and he positioned me and I heard him say, "I just want to feel the outside of you, just a little, just..."

Fuck. My God. It was happening.

"Okay, yes," he said, and entered me.

Two minutes. Three. He pressed against me, and then, when my eyes were closed and my teeth found my bottom lip and I thought I could guess the rhythm that was developing, he was gone, out.

I dropped my legs down and situated my panties as he lay his head down on the couch. I pretended this was all very normal. He breathed hard, and I heard his refrain between breaths.

Oh god oh god oh god.

He looked up at me when I finished zipping up my shorts.

"I think I need some industrial-strength paper towels," he said in a daze, and we laughed, the sound of my own tinkling out of me.

I checked the clock again. He had to go.

He gave me a platonic kiss on the mouth. Hungry, tired, and unsteady, I tried to pull him back for something more substantial, but he chuckled slyly at me and pulled away, as if I had asked for cookies and didn't have any money. I let him go, waved at him as he left through the screen door which I locked behind him. He pulled away in his old green Porsche, one wave, then his eyes were on the road. I briefly glanced at the picture window of the house across the street. The small lamp was on above the easel forever stationed in that window, but there was no one there. I unlocked the screen, and shut the door. Bolted it.

I ran to my room and checked the digital clock. I counted on my fingers the time difference in Germany. I wanted to call Abigail, who was there for the summer, and tell her I had caught up with her. I was the third now among my friends. I stopped in the middle of my room and checked my panties for blood. I was not a virgin anymore.

Before I could make the international call, the phone rang and I ran to the kitchen extension. Maybe it was my mom, telling me she was too tired to go to the store or make dinner, and would I like Kentucky Fried Chicken? I stubbed out the cigarette I was carrying into the kitchen ashtray and waved one arm to spread the smoke around in the air as I picked up the phone.

"It's me," Jeff shouted. There was a steady roar of traffic in the background.

"What's wrong?" I asked, scared, confused.

"I can't believe it," he said. Did I hear disappointment? Regret? Or resignation? I immediately felt like crying, then I steeled myself.

"What? What?" I said. I couldn't think of what else to say.

"I had to pull over on the fucking freeway. I couldn't drive. I felt like I was having a heart attack...Not now, though, but I just needed to stop a minute..."

I was silent, waiting, my forehead furrowed, holding my breath.

"I mean, c'mon, I just committed...I just committed the cardinal sin of teaching, Wendy! The worst thing...I just broke the rules, majorly, and I'm a little sick, I feel crazy..." He trailed off.

I tried to picture exactly where he was calling from, why it was so loud, was he really on the freeway? At one of those emergency call boxes? Was that possible?

"Okay," I said. "It's fine. Everything's okay. I had fun!" Suddenly 'fun' sounded like something a fourteen-year-old would say and I bit my lip. "What—what exactly is making you feel sick?"

"Okay, okay," he answered. "You're not telling a soul, you're not writing a word of this down anywhere, right?"

"Hell no!" I exclaimed. The "hell" sounded shaky. "No one knows anything. I swear!" *Please believe me,* I thought. *Please don't let this be the one and only time.*

"There's nothing to worry about, I promise," I followed up. I listened to him for another two minutes, ranting, raving, until he sounded calmer. He was the teacher I knew again, laughing, witty, making fun of his own overreaction, ready to get back in the Porsche and head to Pasadena.

When we hung up, I glanced at the clock and recalculated the time in Germany.

SUMMER
1987

Puberty in a nutshell: I was regularly high, hormonal and passionately angry. My mother was deep in menopause and recently separated and the infrequent binges I knew from childhood were sorely missed because now she was at full throttle.

My father was becoming a memory who stepped in every once in a while to remind me he was more than a memory.

I awaited nightly the eager-sounding bell on the Princess phone in my bedroom to announce that someone was thinking of me, wanted to hear my voice. If I was sequestered in my room, this could also help avoid an angry collision with my mother, who began her descent into the weekend by six o'clock Friday evening, vodka and orange soda parked next to her, sometimes through Monday.

There was occasional respite from routine. There were Saturdays spent at Venice Beach, when she bought me clothes, colorful patches of peace signs and dancing turtles, translucent stickers and wine coolers, to make up for her being passed out the entire weekend before. I wound my way through stands of colorful clothes, choosing tie-dyes, jeans, Indian print dresses. I was evolving from my cocoon of black and gray clothing, wanting to be clothed in something that shouted my existence and was reminiscent of a more colorful, electric world that I wanted to be a part of.

No one carded me when I was with my mother, ever.

After a movie one Friday evening, my mother drove us to the Hidden Door, a bar by our house. She told me she just wanted one beer, and to come in with her. For fun, I ordered a Corona, and we looked at each other and giggled when the bartender served me. Four beers later, I waltzed to the bathroom, swaying over the toilet, and puked a steady stream of beer and popcorn.

The second time we went to a bar, it was The Townhouse on Venice Beach. The jukebox seemed a novelty to me, and again I was allowed to sit at the bar, smoke, drink alongside my mother. When asked by other bar patrons to shoot a game of pool, my mom nodded at me, as if giving permission, and I played a sloppy game. Someone gave me quarters for the jukebox, and I stood over it, concentrating on the block letters before they escaped me, trying to recall the songs I just decided on. The voice of Madonna lilted through the bar; someone told me I looked like her, and I drunkenly saw the resemblance in the shadowy glass frame of a painting on the dingy brown wall. I danced around the bar to "La Isla Bonita," and no one gave it a second thought. My mother laughed like she enjoyed seeing me happy. Later, I tried to concentrate more on the free feeling I had that afternoon, and less on the feeling that my mother was absolutely batshit bonkers now that we were on our own, without my father to anchor us.

Earlier that day in Venice, I was hanging around one of the "No Nukes" tables on the boardwalk when a guy suddenly said into my ear, "So we're going to coffee, right?"

I looked up. A complete stranger. I laughed and told him I was with my mom.

"It's okay," he said with a smile, and disappeared into the crowded boardwalk. I was suddenly consumed by the innocence of such a flirtation. There was no dirty talk, no intentional brushes against my needy skin. This man, now invisible among the masses, was harmless.

Even as my sandaled feet walked the overcrowded boardwalk, I recognized that I was becoming deeply acquainted with harm, with men in cars that stopped and offered me a ride to wherever I was headed, casually offering wine coolers or pot, if I would do them *just one favor*.

I shook harm's hand, swung open the door, and got in.

1995

Many years later, on a wood floor with several other women, I practiced making a fist.

Even before we practiced making fists, there was a routine I was getting accustomed to with every lesson.

We stretched. We rotated our hips. We took deep breaths. And then we talked about intuition. We talked about our worth.

It seems strange, perhaps, but what a compelling subject. One's worth. Around a bunch of strangers.

What we had in common was that we were women. We were women wanting to learn self-defense. We defined ourselves as feminists and we were processing the notion that in order to defend ourselves we might first have to address our own worth.

This was a radical concept. It was more radical than learning to enter a room and make an escape plan. It was more radical than practicing kicks or jabs or remembering that the eyeballs were an excellent target on an attacker.

I had had glimmers of considering the concept of my own worth, but often my worth had been screwed into an altogether twisted definition that I was presently trying to unravel with a bunch of other women in a room every week.

One woman spoke of sleeping with a knife under her pillow. Another spoke of feeling paralyzed by fear.

I couldn't relate and I could. I was learning in these rooms and in college classrooms the words for the situations I had endured as a teenager. The words still did not roll off my lips but they were becoming more present to me. I may not have known what it was like to feel like you had to sleep with a knife under your pillow, but some part of me knew that if it made this woman feel safe, it was by all means good and right.

During those teenage years my self-worth was something I felt was small enough to hold. It was my pen, my paper and sometimes, maybe, my ability to attract people to me.

In college I began to see how this was a skewed self-concept. The word *boundaries* suddenly entered my consciousness and became a constant topic among women I found myself in groups with. Drawing *boundaries*. Good *boundaries*. The dreaded *bad boundaries*. That was something I knew a lot about.

There were the *womyn*-only spaces and the *wimmin*-only spaces and the bisexual-only spaces and the women-of-color spaces. I conformed to boundaries drawn. I drew boundaries around as much as I could. I was making up for all the boundaries crossed with and without my consent, my thirteen, fourteen, fifteen-year-old "consent," not yet knowing I couldn't totally make up for what was lost.

I listened attentively to discussions about confidence. Assertiveness. I learned the term "self-care." A part of me scoffed but a much bigger part of me knew these were tools I hadn't had, tools to carry forward into a much bigger, more satisfying existence.

I learned to use my feet, my core, my fists. I learned to embody what for years would be a mode of resistance before it could transform into something else.

SUMMER
1987

Most Friday nights, I was homebound—my mother's imposed curfew—and voluntarily holed up in my room, with the occasional foray into the kitchen for snacks: Diet Cokes, popcorn, leftover pizza, chips.

At three in the morning, I turned off the television and closed the blinds. Until sleep caught up to me, the lights were low. The smooth, cream-colored finish of my little-girl bed's headboard gleamed in the light, its etchings of leaves, vines, and tiny flowers not so apparent in the shadows. The bed was covered hastily in one sheet with the scratchy, knobby mattress peeking through the sides where the sheet didn't reach. On top of my mattress, where I preferred less and less to sleep, the springs seemed to issue a constant threat of breaking through.

The bright, wheat-y looking yellow fibers of the carpet bent and swayed in traffic patterns. Later, dark spots would appear here and there, black blobs of hair dye saturating the yellow, marking the decision to go black after a round of orangey bleached hair. There was a cigarette burn or two, because if I was going to have a curfew, I was going to smoke in my room. (The carpet, I later learned, caused rug burns, which I modeled shamelessly in photographs at any given time from the ages of fourteen to eighteen. One photograph, circa 1988, shows me at age fifteen, knees bent displaying rug burns, one hand at my mouth securing a joint, the other making a peace sign. My eyes were scrunched close and the smoke practically wafts off the photo paper.)

Covering both sides of my bedroom door: *Life in Hell* comic strips from the pages of the *L.A. Weekly*; tattered business cards from Poobah's and Moby Disc, record stores I liked to plunder; photos ripped from the pages of *People* magazine of John Belushi, James Dean, Natalie Wood; a shopping bag shouting "Aardvark's Odd Ark" clothing store; pictures from a Disney coloring book that I colored in with old crayons: the queen from Snow White, the evil fairy from Sleeping Beauty, a Cinderella I transformed into a brunette.

My walls were an homage to the music I listened to faithfully from the time I used my first maxi-pad: Danny Elfman of Oingo Boingo, The Police, Siouxsie and the Banshees. Since I started straying into the numbers at the middle of the FM dial, stations that Jeff listened to, lyrics he quoted began appearing on my walls: John Lennon, David Bowie, Jackson Browne. The lyrics, written in marker, framed pictures of Yosemite, culled from a calendar that Jeff gave me when the year was up, the calendar useless.

Books were stacked around my bed according to importance: if they were for school, they were positioned by the phone; if borrowed from friends, they lay next to the bed, with bookmarks stashed between pages. The little-girl dresser, which matched the headboard and two chests of drawers, connected to a desk and three shelves. The various drawers held notebooks, journals, things-to-do lists (which I made every night beginning in fourth grade and kept paper-clipped together), old pens, markers, letters and postcards from Abigail in Germany, green and white hardcover yearbooks, Chuck E. Cheese tokens, dust bunnies, and later, the beginnings of a hidden pot pipe collection, and the occasional small packet of marijuana.

Under the large oval mirror, which came with the bedroom set, there was another short dresser containing foldable clothes and a top drawer I shared with my mom. Old costume jewelry, bobby pins, watches in need of batteries, terrycloth headbands, old makeup and stray hairs filled the top drawer, housed in a plastic compartmentalized case, in a semblance of order. The dresser top was covered with brushes, combs, the makeup of the moment, tiny pieces of paper, written on and torn from corners of notebook pages, matchbooks and cigarettes or their effluvia: crunchy wrapper, foil paper, errant strands of tobacco.

The two top shelves of the largest dresser housed old, cobwebby stuffed animals that my grandmother called "plush toys," the "plush" always more heavily accented. I could always look up to the highest reaches of the dresser and see the crinkled paper of a handmade folder that contained all of my drawings, finger paintings, and stories, from preschool to first grade.

Dust was the patina covering most of the room. It covered the blinds, creating a thin grime on the cord I used to close and open the garish-colored slats. I remembered, from day one, my bitter anger at my parents' decision to replace my curtains with metal blinds. I was all of seven or eight, and they chose what I thought to be, and still maintain, the ugliest color combination imaginable for blinds: a burnt orange, next to a flat brown and metallic green, that when washed, turned a flat silver. I stuck a couple of pieces of gum on the window ledge in protest.

I let clothes heap up around the bed, the dressers, on the closet doorknob. My mother kept some of her clothes in my closet and the floor space was covered by her old high-heeled shoes, my budding collection of boots and sandals and later, fringed knee-high moccasins and platforms. The shelf space was for junk she and I could not bear to sift through and make decisions about: my baby clothes, old records of hers, a couple of wigs she wore before I was born. I often closed the door on this alternate dimension and busied myself with what was tangible and in my line of sight: the books, the ashtray, the carton of Marlboro Reds, the telephone.

I spent the rest of summer splayed out on my bed, contemplating the sky through the blinds, analyzing every song lyric I could make out on the radio, interpreting every night's hours-long phone call with Jeff in myriad ways, and waiting for Abigail, who was finally back from visiting her family in Germany, to knock on my window so I could sprint down the hall to the living room and open the front door for her. One night I was listening to a station that Jeff turned me onto. I was immediately suspicious of the jazz fusion sound and eager to tear it apart because it sounded like elevator music and didn't have voices. But I listened, interested because Jeff was interested. A song finished, one featuring a melancholy piano that made me think of him, and how he'd written songs for piano for his girlfriend.

Sniffing the air absently, I tried to locate the scent he had remarked upon, stunning me with his attention to nuance. He told me that everyone has their own unique scent, and that mine gave him "olfactory orgasms." My legs splayed out, I inhaled and caught a hint of iron, reminding me I needed to change my pad. The blood was welcome this time, for the first time. I pressed my legs together and absently reminded myself to pay close attention to other people's scents, their olfactory imprint, but all I could imagine was the scent of Ralph Lauren Polo on a wooly sweater.

I sat on my bed, still, yet electric, thinking I was in love, staring at the tops of the tree branches that wound their way from the backyard and touched my long, rectangular window.

The sky, I thought, preparing to find a pen and paper, *is a rich hue of violet-blue-gorgeous.* The pine needles wavered in the slight wind of the summer night.

I sat and concentrated hard, picturing not the houses across the street or the freeway behind them, but the ocean. I placed the shore just beyond the trees. The dull roar of the freeway fell away, became the dull roar of ocean waves, and I closed my eyes. I saw myself, shoeless, letting my toes squish in the brown, damp sand, hugging myself against the sea spray. I saw myself, and I was quiet and unnaturally content.

I opened my eyes, untwisted my legs and set them on the carpet. I pulled on a jacket and set out to meet Abigail halfway as she walked from the bus stop in that other world. As I walked, I pictured the salt air and the endless water stretching out, covering the houses, crashing over the freeways, drowning out the voices of men who wish for you not to love them and the sounds of girls crying into pillows, oceans dripping from their eyes.

AUGUST
1987

The days of summer flipped past like the pages of the books I was inhaling. The fan was perpetually on. There was a constant feeling of exhilaration, as if I was an actress on opening night, an opening night that occurred again and again.

The San Fernando Valley in August resembled an oven on broil. Nevertheless, I pulled on my trusty pair of gray wool shorts and a white, sleeveless blouse—tight in the right places, the color a flag of surrender.

I double-checked the phones. I picked each one up from its receiver, listened, and replaced it in its niche. Dial tones.

I called my mom at work to make sure she would be there until 3:30.

"Promise we'll go to the store?" I asked timidly, and she bit the bait, agreed with me in a tired voice that she and I would pick up groceries together. I felt and sounded like the fourteen-year-old girl she knew me to be, though our relationship was plummeting like a car down a cliff in slow motion. I didn't think about this for too long. I hung up the phone and knew I was home free.

I showered and sprayed myself with something in my mother's bathroom that said it smelled like Obsession by Calvin Klein. After a quick flick of the wrist, spray floating gently around me, I walked barefoot into the living room and reclined on the mottled sofa. After scooting down to the side my mother favored, I was within reach of her pack of golden Marlboros. I enjoyed a leisurely cigarette, the smoke wafting out the locked screen. I crossed and recrossed my legs.

Aware of my bouncing leg and the rush of the nicotine entering my bloodstream, I stood and approached the front door. Through the dusty screen I could see the neighbors' houses. In the house across the street, the one with the easel in the front window, the curtains were open wide. I was used to seeing the man who lived there; he watered his lawn pathologically in the afternoons. Sometimes, he and the woman who lived with him painstakingly cleaned the old, beautiful cars in their garage and driveway. I made up stories about them. She looked so much younger than him from where I was standing, I could swear that she and I had something in common. The stories sometimes involved me, and how the man might invite me into his house, drawing the curtains shut. (Years later, I would stand on his doorstep, and he would allow me entrance. They would prove themselves a charming and eccentric couple, and we would share a short, strange conversation as he sat in his antique dentist's chair in the living room, cuddling a skull. "Robert Williams," I would explain to my mother later in a Hollywood art gallery, "He's this crazy artist, check out his paintings.") But none of this was revealed to me on this day. His curtains were simply open and there was no sight of him, just the ghostly form of the large white easel in the corner of the picture window.

I savored each day I was still free from school. I woke up late, to the sound of the phone, my mother calling from work to growl at me to awaken and do some chores. Sometimes she sounded bored and girlish, wanting to chat. I relished each day that she left at six-thirty in the morning. I ruled the house until I heard the click-clack of her heels marching up the concrete walkway at four.

Every day I listened to my mother's ongoing litany on the importance of keeping the door shut and bolted. If that was not possible due to the heat, the need for air circulation, I should at least remember to lock the screen.

Remembering this, I checked the lock on the screen.

I went back to the couch and reclined, feeling the slight breeze hit my bare shoulders, legs.

When I heard his Porsche pull up, I jumped. I threw myself back onto the couch but leaned forward and strained my eyes to make sure I could see the green vehicle parked in front of my house. When he started his way up the walk, I got up to unlock the screen. He was already at the door, peering in, touching the screen. He banged on it a couple of times so that I leapt to open it, and he entered, loud and sweet, calling out for my mom, my dad, the FBI, anyone to come on out and catch him.

I laughed and closed the heavy door behind him. Shut. Bolted.

There was an aura of danger we created, accompanied by perfect release. He barely kissed me but let his lips and tongue linger over my neck, my cheek, my chest. I leaned back on my mother's couch and closed my eyes, fearful that eye contact would remind him that I was still fourteen and he was nearing twenty-nine.

We eagerly unbuttoned my shorts.

"Why the hell do you wear these all the time, do you know it's a hundred degrees out?" he asked me. I wrapped my calves up against his thick neck in response.

There would be no penetration this time. I began to understand that it might never happen again, based on clues such as Jeff's comfort level, his day at work, the potential for paranoia to strike after he ventured into my bedroom and was reminded I was a girl and not a woman.

So I remained, sighing against him, my heated breathing attempting to match his, attempting to keep us deep in the fantasy, deep in a charged, thick miasma of denial.

~

I knew on one particular night in August that if my phone rang, it would not be Jeff's voice.

He and his on-again, off-again girlfriend were going to a concert at Anaheim Stadium. David Bowie, my longtime idol, was headlining, with Siouxsie and the Banshees opening.

Jealousy clouded my vision, imagining Jeff and his girlfriend at the stadium. I told myself that they could probably not even appreciate the brilliant spectacle that was Siouxsie Sioux. Fucking straights. Old, I thought, he is old, too old to appreciate this.

Siouxsie's lyrics were emblazoned on my closet door in blue marker:

> The stars that shine
> And the stars that shrink
> In the face of stagnation
> The water runs
> Before your eyes...

I turned my stereo on, loud, turning the dial until I found the station I listened to most.

I heard the oceanic sound of a crowd cheering, a person on microphone. They were broadcasting live from Anaheim Stadium. The radio was bringing me to Jeff and his girlfriend. I imagined them probably stoned, and excited, and laughing in the midst of thousands of people shouting, stamping their feet, waving lighters, focused on the stage.

I stretched out on my bedroom floor and let the tears sting my eyes. My knees were raw and I heard a crack in my kneecap. I sat up quickly, blood rushing to my head. I crawled to the closet, pulled open the door, and let my hand run across the old backpacks and overnight bags on the floor until I found the heavy one, the one that concealed wine coolers and dank clothing to smother the clinking of bottles.

I lie back again on the carpet, careful to leave the opened Bartles and James behind the chair should my mother barge in. My mother had bought them in a moment of poor judgment, because she knew she wouldn't touch them, and didn't believe I would. They were confiscated when she left for work, and she never inquired of them again.

The crowd built to a climactic cheer.

I saw Mr. Ivers in my mind's eye, with the woman I'd only seen photos of, a petite, busty woman with dark skin and curly black hair and a Persian name. The tears stopped abruptly, and I was left with a thought.

You're a kid. A child. Not a woman. A girl. Not a girlfriend.

I sat up and took a long, hard swallow of the watermelon-tasting alcohol and set it down, keeping my hand around its body, fingering the torn label on the glass.

> *Swallowing diamonds*
> *A cutting throat*
> *Your teeth when you grin*
> *Reflecting beams on tombstones...*

•

Goddamn him.

My body felt hot and prickly. If someone touched me, I thought I might explode into a million needles.

My head throbbed with a mantra.

I hurt I hurt I hurt.

Meanwhile, Anaheim Stadium was treated to the words on my wall, the beautiful confluence of orchestral maneuver and goth-voice of Siouxsie.

Would he remember that I have these words on my wall? Would he maybe think of me?

These questions deserved a swig of sickly sweet wine cooler. And another.

A jamboree of surprises
Playing Russian roulette
Or the lucky clip
A clenched fist to your heart
Coal dust on your lungs

I squeezed my eyes shut until my eyeballs ached.

I fumbled for the pack of Marlboros under the bed with its companions, ashtray and lighter.

A silver tongue for the chosen one
Heavy magnum in your side
Or a bloody thorn

This is bullshit, I thought. *Here I am, fourteen. Cute (enough). Smart (enough). Right?*

There was no answer.

I was wasting hours of my life pining away for this man that taunted me with his sexual innuendos. He tormented me with descriptions of the loud, jubilatory, reunited sex he and his girlfriend had, because, well, it had been soooo long. And, he told me, he knew it wouldn't work out between them. But still he loved her.

Skating bullets on angel dust
In a dead sea of fluid mercury,
Baby piano cries, under your heavy
Index and thumb
Pull some strings—LET THEM SING
I smoked the cigarette hurriedly, hungrily. My nostrils flared.

The three of us, and all of Anaheim Stadium, and every person in Southern California who touched their radio dial and listened to this wailing, melancholy, beautiful voice—I thought everyone was witness to my error, my belief that I was worthy of this person's love. Worthy of anyone's love.

Dazzle

It's a glittering prize

Clenched muscles. Tightened forehead. I scrunched my eyes shut and concentrated.

If I have a goddamn telepathic molecule in this body, just one, let me use it NOW, like FIRE beating its path to him...Jeff, you are fucking HURTING me and I love you like I have never loved anyone.

Siouxsie kept on.

The stars that shine,

And the stars that shrink...

NOTES ON AN EXCAVATION:

WHY I DIDN'T TELL

I didn't want to be average.

I didn't want it to end.

I was comfortable keeping secrets.

I was afraid of being blamed.

I felt responsible for his acts.

I was numb.

I was told I exuded sex and therefore I must be to blame.

The truth is, I did tell.

I didn't want it to end.

I told an adult.

I grew comfortable with anguish. With hostility.

Tragedy.

I was numb.

That adult has since apologized for his inaction on my behalf, shared with me his fear of the situation, his own newness to the profession at the time.

I imagined courtrooms. Lawyers pointing at me. A brief on all my sexual exploits passed around, read aloud.

I was ashamed, so much so that I wasn't sure I could live through something like that.

There were plenty of signs but I did not have parents who were capable of interpreting those signs.

I thought it was my karma.

There was even a social worker.

I get numb, still, thinking about this question.

I wanted sex.

I wanted to be the focal point of someone's world.

When the social worker indicated that what I was talking about might be reportable, I left and never went back.

I wanted power.

I fight numbness regularly.

I thought there was something to learn from this.

I wanted love.

It would be years later that I would tell and tell and tell in a room, rooms a thousand miles north of where it all happened.

It's like walking around a live mine. Say the wrong thing, move the wrong way, there could be casualties.

What would you say to a girl if you suspected something? Were told something?

I would ask careful, simple questions, after I listened.

How does he treat you?

What do you feel in his presence?

Where do the feelings go in your body when he's not around?

Why is it a secret? What do you have to gain by keeping it a secret? And what do you have to lose?

SEPTEMBER 1987

Jeff picked me up on the street outside Notre Dame's gates on a shortened class day.

He had not yet started his own school year; my new Catholic high school started in late August.

I wore the uniform I purchased three weeks before while obliterated on rum and Coke. I had to hold the bag between my body and the boy whose motorcycle I was riding on the back of. After that day, I could never drink rum again.

"So, I have this personal problem," Jeff said as I climbed into his Porsche. He spoke again when we were blocks away from my school.

"I'll show you," he said, and steered us down a cul-de-sac. After a quick glance around, he unzipped his pants. My breath caught, unsure of what was happening. I looked down briefly at a patch of flesh, and then up, staring through the windshield. My teeth bit into the soft insides of my mouth.

"While I was on vacation I fucked around with some twenty-year-old chick and I think she gave me something I'd rather not have. So I'm out of commission for awhile. Sorry to get your hopes up."

"It's okay," I said, rearranging myself on the small seat. I looked forward, aware of the wool herringbone skirt on my thigh, my white blouse blazing in the sun. I felt a little sick. A swarm of bees entered my head, agitated. I tried to make my mouth smile.

"Let's just drive around." He motioned at the sky. "It's beautiful out."

Hansen Dam looked like death. I saw no water. My white anklet socks and my new burgundy penny loafers got covered in dust. I put a finger to my tongue and bent down to shine the pennies in their slits.

"A hawk!" Jeff called out.

We'd been standing apart for minutes. *Fucked around. Twenty-year-old chick.* I took a deep breath and looked into the sky. The sun beat down on my face, and I raised a hand to shield my eyes from the sun. A hawk circled the air high above us.

I looked back at Jeff. His posture was in reverence to the hawk, amazed and grateful. I watched them both and felt a slight smile. I blinked and put my hands on my hips, silent.

He kissed me goodbye when we arrived at the gas station near my house.

"Can I have another?" I asked in my version of sweetness. I lifted a knee and my skirt rode higher on my leg. I picked up my bag from the floor of the car.

"Nope. Sorry."

My face crumpled before I could control myself. Before I knew it, words were spilling out.

"Just once, just once when I ask you for one, I hope you'll give it to me!"

I paused for effect. I flung open the door, stepped out, slammed the door shut. I felt my skirt swish around the back of my thighs, where I hoped his eyes would travel. I started walking towards my house, each step heavy, forced, the muscles in my calves straining. He pulled out and sped away.

My phone rang at 10:30 that night.

"What you said earlier. You were right. And for your information, I almost turned around and drove back."

We talked until morning.

He loved the poems I wrote for him. I tried to get a word in edge-wise about high school, my freshman classes, my uncomfortable uniform, the senior boys who were so cute.

"*Please* don't talk about other guys. I don't wanna hear it," he said, and my heart opened. I found it. A tender spot, a soft place I could put a finger on until it hurt both of us.

After we hung up, I fell asleep, satiated, forgetting about the need for kisses.

～

High school was unlike anything I had ever imagined. It certainly did not resemble anything I'd seen on television. The high school-aged boys and girls I met at the Galleria, or through Veronica's skinhead and punk channels, didn't speak of, or attend, high school, which made "high school" seem like a parallel universe. The worst part was that Veronica was at another high school across the Valley. Abigail was at mine, and so were most of my friends from junior high and elementary school.

There were mandatory religion classes for each of the four years. Electives consisted of speech class, business law, art and art history, and few others. I marveled as students drove into the school parking lot, slid their cars into a space, hung out until the first bell rang.

For the first time ever, Abigail and I walked past each other into separate classrooms every day, waving hello, a palpable electricity in the air between us as the unspoken was acted out: a different configuration of the triangle had come into existence. I was more Veronica's friend now, even though she was at a different school. I neither questioned nor concerned myself with this new development.

And there were other new things. One day at school, I noticed Dennis Monroe.

"Okay," our teacher said. "We're going to take ten minutes for some lucky people to prepare a debate. What are some topics?" he inquired of the class.

Speech class was composed of students from every grade. Dennis Monroe was a senior, drove an orange Volkswagen bus, and had the dubious title of "yell leader," which was related somehow to cheerleading. I kept my eyes averted from the senior cheerleaders on game days, when their blue and gold skirts barely covered their butts, their sweaters unnaturally tight. Dennis Monroe seemed the safest bet for a public crush.

My infatuation was clinched in speech class.

"How about men versus women? Let's have a debate on who's superior: men or women," someone called out.

The class stirred in their seats, people laughing and chewing out loud on this topic. We waited expectantly while students were chosen to participate, and ten minutes later, the debate began.

A young woman stood up and described the nurturing capabilities of women, their love of peace, their common-sense attitude. Her skirt almost touched her knees and I made a mental note to have mine shortened. We listened attentively, courteously, as she continued her argument.

"And that's why women will always be superior to men," she said in closing. She turned and looked smugly at Dennis Monroe, who stood at the lectern next to hers.

He looked down at the paper on his lectern, hiding what appeared to be a smile. I watched his down-turned head, his thick, black hair that looked a little long for the school's rules. He looked up, treating us to his hazel-green eyes and smattering of freckles.

"Women," he said, his deep voice rousing my insides, "are indeed deserving of worship."

Our class looked at him and at each other in amusement. Our teacher looked as if he might stop him mid-sentence. I stared at Dennis's face, eager to hear what he was getting at, how he might hijack speech class.

"For one, they are remarkable, physiologically. Way more attractive than men."

The class tittered. I laughed out loud and covered my mouth with a nervous hand.

"And secondly," he paused, his face contorting from smile to straight line, "they are multi-orgasmic. Who else can accomplish such a feat? Men can't. Women, on the other hand, can have several orgasms within a matter of minutes..." he trailed off as kids shrieked, laughing. Three leaps and our teacher was in front of the class, red-faced and smiling nervously. "That's quite enough, quite enough," he said, and then, "Let's get a different example, shall we?"

I watched Dennis saunter back to his seat. His shirt was untucked and his khakis loose. I allowed my body to feel the heat of early-crushhood, the prickly feeling of wanting someone's lips all over me, tasting the salty spots, lingering on the soft, secret places.

Speech class became my favorite hour of the day.

After that day, I talked about my crush on Dennis with Jeff as often as I could. It seemed to cause a small commotion whenever I mentioned it, inflaming our visits which resumed, girlfriend or not.

FALL
1987

My destination most Saturdays, bus pass in hand, was the Four and Twenty Restaurant in Van Nuys. The bus dropped me off near the restaurant, before the long walk down a suburban cluster of houses that all looked alike. No one seemed to stand outside these houses, washing their cars out front, or even peeking out the curtains. I felt invisible and yet slightly important walking the sidewalks to Jeff's house, if I was granted a visit.

Back at the Four and Twenty, before I could even begin my march, I had to deposit twenty cents into the public phone, press the buttons, wait for the cue. His voice came on the line and I put on my sassy tone, the one that seemed to get me the most from the situation at hand. I told him where I was and in the silence after I said it, I could feel whether or not a visit was in store.

I never knew who might be at his house on a Saturday. The call was a requirement, a signal. Sometimes I waited in the coffee shop, nibbling at a slice of key lime pie, sipping coffee, until I could call at the agreed-upon hour later, when he might be alone again.

On his bed, I watched myself in the mirror as I straddled him, the herringbone skirt I'd carried in my backpack for this occasion hiked around my hips, contemplating what he saw in me, what Dennis Monroe might see in me, or anyone for that matter.

I returned home in the late afternoon or early evening. I told my mother about my trip to the library, the record store, friend's houses—if and when she was sober enough to ask, to listen.

Monday morning came and I listened as my friends talked about their weekends. I listened quietly, laughed at the right moments, asked clarifying questions attentively.

I did not bring up my weekends, how drunk I was, how late I stayed out, or who I hitched a ride from.

When asked about my weekend, I condensed Saturday and Sunday into something that sounded legal. *What they don't know won't hurt them*, I thought passively as I watched Dennis Monroe standing outside his bus on Monday mornings, as I listened to stories of dinner with parents, PG movies, and Catholic school carnivals.

~

One Saturday, we made plans to see each other at my old school, the one where we'd met, so that I could help him put up some calendars and posters in his classroom.

I arrived at my junior high campus later than I hoped, feeling a little older and wiser now that I was down the street at high school.

Jeff was nowhere to be seen and the front gate of the school was locked. I stood around waiting, glaring at the cars passing, wanting to not appear like I was looking for a ride, or eager, or as angry as I felt for being stood up.

An hour later I saw his car. I felt like I had a tightly strung wire running up my back and the sight of his car made it snap deliciously.

All anger and impatience was forgotten. After unlocking the gate, he drove his car into the parking lot and we walked to his classroom.

"Ready to work?" he asked me, rubbing his palms together.

"Well..." I began, unsure about the extent I was willing to work on a Saturday, wondering what he meant, exactly, by "work."

"C'mon," he goaded. "There's something in it for you." He rustled through his backpack. He opened it wide enough so that I could see a single Seagram's wine cooler inside.

"Alright then," I said, and we commenced hanging posters on the walls with heavy-handed blows to staplers and thumbs pressed firmly on the golden heads of tacks.

We talked while situating the posters and photos on the bulletin boards. In the midst of the conversation, we argued, a recent but not uncommon occurrence. Needled by talk of flirtations with other women, I became silent, seething.

"What's up? Why aren't you talking?" he asked.

I shook my head. I had already gulped down the wine cooler and smoked my cigarette out on the street in front of the campus. The tears were building behind my eyes.

"You know, Wendy, this is fucking annoying. Your silent treatment is getting a little old." He paused to look me in the face. I stared past him at the chalkboard, a replica of who I had tried to become in his classroom. Disinterested. Unshakeable.

"You should be an actress," he continued, an edge in his voice. "You can make your face so blank, I can't tell what you're thinking."

Silence.

"You know what? This is worthless." He turned his back to me and continued organizing the papers on his desk.

A ripple of fury traveled up and down my skin.

"Worthless," I repeated. I stood up, grabbed my bag and stomped out. As I left the classroom, a disturbing hope bloomed in me: the wish that he was watching me, the way my hair swung around my face dramatically, the way my body vibrated with heat and anger. I imagined the specks of color in the linoleum dashing around, searching for safety under the power of my boots.

"Are you really leaving?" he called out to me.

"Does it look like I'm faking it?" I asked.

The bus uncannily appeared moments after I arrived at the bus stop, and I boarded, heading back down Woodman Avenue to my house. After a cigarette and the short walk from the bus stop to my house, I felt the pressure leave my temples. Gripping the house keys in one hand, my backpack in the other, I unlocked the deadbolt and stepped inside.

A sour smell greeted me. The stereo was blaring and my mother was passed out on the couch, her mouth open, snoring. Her drink sat half empty on the glass coffee table, moisture around its base.

I tiptoed to the dining room table and slowly removed her wallet from her purse. I pressed it to my hip and entered the kitchen. The music enveloped all of the usual creaks and groans of the house, most of which I memorized in order to leave quietly when the stereo was off and I had to make a getaway while my mother was unconscious.

I rifled through her wallet. It smelled of worn leather and cigarettes, a hint of perfume and the soft scent of powder. My fingers touched several tens, a few fives and some tattered ones. I decided on a five and a one, snapped its clasp together and slipped the wallet back into her purse.

Less than two hours later I was back at the gates of my old junior high.

I called out over the ivy-covered fence and Jeff heard me from his seat on the wooden bench on the basketball courts. When he unlocked the gate, I could see Louis, the maintenance man, with him. They were in the middle of passing a pipe back and forth.

I acted casual and sat down on the concrete, listening to them finish their conversation, keeping my eyes off the shared pipe. I courageously fished out my cigarettes and lit one, not looking at Jeff's face. I grabbed an empty Sprite can from underneath the bench and delicately tipped my ashes inside, staring at the green and gold can as I did so, careful not to let my eyes rest anywhere else.

"This is some good stuff," Jeff said, standing up, stretching his arms above his head. "Wendy's cool," he said to Louis, who nodded and eyed me. I noted the dimple in his cheek and looked back down at the Sprite can. Jeff reached into his jeans pocket and produced an aluminum foil packet.

"Here. For helping me out with the classroom. Don't smoke it all in one place."

I thanked him and put the foil in my backpack. Louis chuckled and walked away, leaving us alone on the courts. After an uncomfortable silence, we walked over to the thick-trunked tree that stood as sentry to the campus.

I threw my backpack on the concrete and hoisted myself up on the first branch. Throwing my leg up, I pulled myself up to a perch. The ridges of the trunk and branches were soft and yielding, while their collective thickness seemed impossible to penetrate. From where I sat, one arm latched around a branch level with my head, I could see Woodman Avenue over the ivy-covered fence, and the lit entrance to the apartments across the street.

The wind was chilly and I realized I forgot to bring a sweater. The wind seared my skin, my skin that felt flush, alive. I admired my arm as it held the tree, the contours of skin wrapped over bone and muscle, the undersides of my arm desperately pale from lack of sun. It was nearly five, and the sun was lost behind clouds, night approaching. I looked down and Jeff and Louis were standing there, looking up at me. Jeff laughed when I noticed them.

"Are you sniffing glue? What are you doing up there?" he called.
"You better not be dropping acid or something," Louis said with a smooth smile.

"Look, we need to head out," Jeff said. "I can give you a ride home, but you need to give me the little present back."

I sighed. I climbed down, trying to infuse a certain prowess to each decision I made as I carefully removed myself from the tree. I produced the packet from my backpack and handed it over. Louis stood by, shaking his large key ring. I nimbly climbed back up the tree as they joked around, saying goodbye in voices I couldn't hear from my branch.

When Louis's car pulled out of the lot and the gate was locked, Jeff climbed up into the tree with me. We sat in silence as the cars shot by on Woodman and the bus made its lumbering stop and lurched forward again towards Ventura Boulevard.

"Are we going to be friends for life?"

His voice sounded open, childlike, strange. I felt him looking up at me from his lower branch. I stared out into the sky, wishing all the artificial lights would go out so I could see as many stars as possible. I imagined him looking at me and reading my thoughts, seeing through me to the other side, his reluctant awareness that I might love him.

I looked down at him briefly and gave him a smile. Goosebumps congregated on my arms and my ass hurt from sitting on the branch. I swung my legs.

"I hope so," I said finally.

Jeff's face was still upturned, searching me, and I realized I was tired. Too tired to act sexy, too tired to flex or pout or fight. The night was open, empty. There was not a home I wanted to go to, but I didn't know what I wanted either. Each thought seemed to require a massive feat of concentration, force, and energy, none of which I had. The boulevard started to look watery, blurred. I looked up the expanse of the tree, what was left to climb, and willed my chest to stillness, my eyes to dryness.

We eventually climbed down. Sitting by the steps of a classroom, I listened to Jeff's mouth work as he chewed tobacco. I had to grow accustomed to this tobacco-chewing, which was new to me and only reminded me that his mouth was generally unavailable for kissing.

"Are you sure nothing's wrong?" he asked me for the zillionth time. "You're not taking any weird drugs I should know about?"

My face didn't change. "Nope. Nothing."

It was officially night. I had a fleeting thought of home as I stepped into his car, how my mom might awaken and find I wasn't there. How she might hurriedly get in her car and go looking for me, as she had done a few times before, always sure to make a stop at the liquor store on the way.

Jeff locked the gate behind his rumbling Porsche and got back inside the car. He let the car idle, watching the traffic go by. I snuck a look at his face. The headlights of approaching cars lit up his cheek, ruddy and soft-looking. He turned to me.

"Let's take a drive," he said.

I felt a sense of being placated, his tone deferential and warm. The car was suddenly on Woodman and I was staring straight ahead into the night, tasting the freedom this kind of night allowed me to have, something heavy, thick, deep. I flexed my fingers, wishing I could take hold of this freedom in my hands. Keep it.

We sailed through the hills past Ventura Boulevard. We went up winding, sloping roads that made me catch my breath. I'd never seen them at night. He parked the car off a small dirt road, unnamed, lacking signage, one of the many secrets of Mulholland.

The silence was loud, as if conversations were flowing so fast they'd reached a drone, a din drowning itself out. We said nothing, while words, sentences formed in my head. I was too scared to put the words together and speak them.

When he leaned over to kiss me I knew it was only to cheer me up, to break the silence.

He started the car again and we made our way back to the lights of Ventura Boulevard.

"Don't take me home yet."

He sighed, turned left on Ventura, and we headed towards the west Valley, which always felt far from home.

The next time we pulled over, there was kissing, and small noises that came from my throat. I imagined the words I wanted to say lodged there, my mouth becoming more heavy with every kiss, every grope. Parked in a grove of trees, unsure of where we were, I had my first orgasm in Jeff's presence. I could see the moon. My hand grasped the door frame of the Porsche and I closed my eyes, knowing his eyes were on my face. I didn't want him to see me cry.

Then the night was shooting by again, the cars blazing on either side of us, the stoplights frantically changing from red to green. My stomach growled and I absently replaced an errant bra strap to my shoulder. I tried to see my reflection in the passenger side window without Jeff noticing.

The long brick building that housed a cookie factory and the beige Anheuser Busch brewery flew past. I wondered if I was beautiful or if my exhaustion, which I felt in every pore, was seeping through so that Jeff could see. I gave up concentrating on the reflection and stared ahead in silence.

As he drove down Roscoe Boulevard heading ever closer to my house, to my mother who would doubtless be overcome with drunken concern and righteous anger, he started talking about his girlfriend. I looked out the window as restaurants, car dealerships, houses, apartments, became a smear of lights. Strong, nauseating smells of grease and hops filled the air and I wished I was walking, somewhere unknown, somewhere far away. My mind flashed on the grove of trees we'd parked under and I wondered if I would ever see them again, if they were on any map I might ever come across.

He parked at the gas station. I opened the door without rolling the window back up. Before he could pull away, I leaned in on the window ledge and my eyes met his.

"I must have set myself up for heartbreak. I knew the whole deal with your girlfriend was inevitable," I heard myself say. I felt like I was standing nearby, watching myself, amazed that I could say such a thing, the unspeakable. I flashed forward in my head to the next phone call, when I might have to apologize, or rationalize my candid remarks, and a new lump lodged in my throat.

He leaned across the seat and held my gaze, his mouth open ever so slightly.

"If you tell me you never want to talk to me again," he said slowly, "that will break my heart."

He turned and stared out the windshield of his car for a moment, and I wondered if he was looking for his own reflection until he spoke again.

"Can you promise me we'll still be friends years from now?"

I turned and looked down the street. The stoplight turned green. Cars careened by, people going on dates, stereos happily vibrating the joys of Saturday night. My legs felt like the asphalt the cars were treading on—heavy, fissured, at some breaking point.

"You can't, can you?" he said finally.

I shook my head, my cheekbones twitching under the pressure of keeping my face from crumpling. He looked down at the seat for a moment, then rolled up his window.

I began the walk home. It was eleven at night. I knew it was possible I'd have some explaining to do when I walked through the front door, which seemed a sick, ridiculous fate.

LATE FALL
1987

One Saturday of many I arrived at his house. I timidly peered through the dusty screen.

"Come on in!"

I opened the screen door and saw him. My attention, my intuition, my conscious, my unconscious seemed entirely in service to this relationship as I stepped through the doorway. I became focused on Jeff's movements, the words that came out of his mouth, what I felt or heard between the lines of conversation until I walked out the screen door again, hips purposely swinging, back to the boulevard.

"Bus stop Wendy, she's here calling," Jeff sang at me to the tune of a song on the oldies station. I stepped into the living room and smiled.

"Well, this time I hitchhiked," I offered by way of conversation.

"You what? *You what? What in the...*"

His hands, which had been packing a tight little wad of pot into a slim pipe, suddenly stopped. I watched the scene unfold, still standing in his living room, letting my backpack drop to the carpet.

"The bus was..."

"No. No. No." He paused. "You know what?" He looked down at the floor, then up at me. My face turned red, a heat I couldn't control traveling from my cheeks and forehead to the tender parts of my ears. My mouth was open, readying for protest, but nothing came out.

"If you need to hitchhike to get here, I'd rather you not come over."

I closed my mouth and swallowed quietly. I moved to pick up my bag. I felt my nostrils flare.

"No, no, wait a minute. Just stay." Jeff's face changed, and he patted the sofa seat next to him. "Here, look, I found a little something in this vial. You want some water? Wanna stay a bit?"

I threw my bag down and sat in one of the dining room chairs, far from the couch he was sitting on. I could see a scar on his knee, his leg hairs creeping out from underneath his shorts.

"Over here," he sang apologetically. He went back to loading the pipe. I sighed loudly and moved to the couch. He set the pipe down and tipped a few drops of water from a glass into a small amber vial that sat on the table.

"Drink it," he said. "It's just a little coke. Probably won't do much."

I took the tiny vial and with the swiftness of a shot of hard liquor I tossed it back. The granules burned my throat. After two hits of pot, I was soothed, though my heart pounded. The anger I'd felt dissipated. I was intent on following the conversation, whether it was about cars or psychiatrists as portrayed on television or the writing of cheap romance novels or hiking the Santa Monica Mountains, the random and mysterious breadth of our conversations while high.

I never took in the details of each room in his house. I rarely ventured into the bedrooms: the risk of being in a room with him not in line of sight of the front door or window was too dangerous.

Once, we ventured into one of his housemate's rooms, where he pointed out a stack of pornography that made me wrinkle my nose even as I wanted to thumb through the pages without anyone else around. We converged in his tiny bathroom, my hands gripping the sink as he entered me, our faces glistening and panting in the mirror on the days when his roommates had all-weekend alibis. I secretly harbored a weird pride that we were the first to "break-in" the rental house, when it was naked and open, void of furniture, like an empty carpeted canvas that we could stain. The house, which was far from being mine, already contained secret memories of our relationship.

I was a guest in his house. Sometimes I was one of many guests, such as the coaches from Oakcrest and Louis the maintenance man. I was expected to come into the house, make myself comfortable, get my own water from the kitchen, and yet I was always rooted to the couch or the chair. I suffered from a strange immobility upon arriving, as if any slight movement would remind Jeff I was really there, only fourteen years old, and therefore must leave. The pendulum then swung in the opposite direction: I moved about, especially if we were alone, in order to maximize the impact of my cut-off shorts, my flimsy white t-shirt with lace bra underneath. I'm here! I wanted to remind him, even as I wished for invisibility. The room often felt pregnant with the reason why I was there, the need.

I now recognize the amalgamation of furniture common to those in their twenties who collect furnishings from garage sales, Dumpsters, their friends' or parents' living rooms. There was a large, bland sofa and a glass dining room table reminiscent of the 1970s, with four matching chairs. There was a mantel holding candles, souvenirs from places traveled, a framed photo of his girlfriend, and a black and white photograph of me, unframed, taken by a yearbook photographer at a junior high school dance.

The living room also featured a built-in bookcase that I often stood in front of, fingering the spines of the paperbacks and hard-covers it held. Its location behind the front door functioned as a place to caress, grope and squeeze, the door wide open, our bodies writhing in view of any person approaching the front steps through the miniature windows of the door hinges. Silent except for the sound of birds chirping outside, he could grab me around the waist with his thick palms and press himself against me as I lay my hands on his forearms, absorbing the energy, the distinct flame of power and arousal between us. If a car pulled up, the flame was doused as quickly as it was lit. I returned to fingering the books on the shelf, situating my mind and my clothes nervously, while he dashed to the other side of the kitchen counter. The sounds from outside had the power to put out the flame that left me aching, ready to start anew, while Jeff was anxious and fidgety, ready to smoke a bowl or do another line.

~

A chilly afternoon passed in fits and starts. One of his housemates had been holed up in his room, thwarting any plans Jeff and I might have had to press ourselves against each other. I knew Jeff's girl-friend lurked in his present life somewhere, but he had stopped mentioning her, only to touch my skin, kiss my mouth, then pull away, saying, "No. I can't."

"Will you give me a ride home?" I asked petulantly, expecting another "no."

I was still surprised as we drove down Van Nuys Boulevard, the sidewalks heaving with people in the midst of the winter holidays. We passed the thrift stores I shopped at regularly, and the Thrifty's drugstore where I bought makeup, and the head shop I had plans to visit. At the stoplight he leaned over and kissed me deeply, once, twice, three times, his free hand touching my cheek, until I could only stare at him in surprise as he returned to the wheel. It was as if his paranoia vanished, replaced with a vulnerable passion I had never seen in him before.

"I'm shopping for your Christmas present," he said.

I couldn't help but beam. "You don't have to."

He smiled.

Kisses in front of the three men who were standing at the bus stop. More kisses goodbye as I left his car, stepping out onto the blacktop of the gas station. The men hooted at our display. I sauntered home, dreaming, tripping occasionally on the buckled sidewalk.

NOTES ON AN EXCAVATION:

1993-2001

Thank *gods* for the experience of college and the life of the town surrounding it.

I am forever indebted to the radicals, queers, faeries, activists, tough girls, strong girls, butch girls, strippers, writers, painters, photographers, and dreamers I came into contact with. It was when I was running with this crowd that I learned the most about my worth.

In college, I met women who wanted to photograph me nude because I wasn't perfect. I met and shared beds with people committed to fighting injustice in smart and sexy ways. I would meet women who had been subjected to the worst kinds of treatment and survived and made their experiences into art.

I learned about love that was not like the love I had been taught in my relationship with Jeff.

Those college years were less about excavation and more about preservation. They were about assessing all that I contained and what could be burnished to the full beauty of its potential.

In therapy rooms around downtown Olympia, Washington, I contemplated the eventual excavation, and later, when it began, I was able to use my brain, my eyes, my hands. I got dirty with the tools and plunged body first into the experience.

And I learned to not let the dirt swallow me whole.

OCTOBER 1987

Saturdays felt like worlds I created once I left the space of my mother's house.

Coming down from a spectacular high that lasted all afternoon, we were rooting around in Jeff's garage. He was pointing out items to me, items of sentimental value that had found a temporary home in the garage before they could be sorted and arranged in the house. Jeff's Siamese cat languidly walked in and around the piles of stuff—junk in my estimation. Her fur touched our legs in small caresses while I tried to concentrate on Jeff's voice, wanting to appreciate his junk as much as he did.

A car pulled up. I felt my head slowly turn and my mouth open, wanting to alert Jeff, who was still on a monologue about another old treasure in a dusty corner of the garage. He heard the car as soon as my head turned.

"Hey, it's Fara," he said calmly.

She got out of the car. I was planted in the cement.

We were introduced.

Fara appeared trim, manicured, hair gelled into place. Her skirt and short-sleeved pastel-colored blouse were well-fitting, bordering on tight. I eyed the gold necklace that hung around her neck, and the wispy bracelet on her wrist, aware that these were gifts.

She smiled and took my hand, said hello in a courteous manner. My cut-off jeans felt stiff against my thighs, my knees locked and naked but for the rough spots that were newly scabbed from rubbing against the carpet in ecstasy. My chest caved in a little, my breasts suddenly feeling pointy and odd in the presence of her filled-up blouse. I noticed I was taller than her. I stood in my tie-dyed Converse high tops across from her white pumps for a few minutes, until it felt safe enough to leave.

"But you don't have to leave," Jeff said, moving next to her and taking her hand.

"No, I do. I've gotta go. Thanks, for everything," I said, moving backward. "Oh, my backpack," I remembered aloud and pointed to his screen. "Can I go in and get it?"

They stood there staring at me. Jeff's face twitched and he said, "Yeah, Wendy, of course. Sure you have to go so soon?"

I caught his drift. Make it seem like I just got there, perhaps.

"Yep, gotta go. Bye. Have fun." My high tops beat a path out of the suburban world, back to the boulevards and buses that might take me somewhere completely different.

~

I managed not to call him that night or the next. My mother complained about the incessant ringing of the phone, and I explained it was probably Abigail, whom she knew I was spending less and less time with. In disgust, I finally unplugged the phones.

When I inserted the plugs back into their square homes, I listened to the messages collect on my answering machine. In one,

Jeff's voice called out, "Hello, this is the fuckhead. Call me back." My finger hit the button. *Erase.*

I finally picked up the phone a few days later.

"I was so worried." I heard a desperate tone in his voice that I liked, a tone that made my hips feel like they were opening up. "That day you took off, Fara and I had to go to dinner in Anaheim and I was nervous and jittery the whole time. Worried about you. Why'd you run off like that? We almost went out looking for you."

I didn't answer. I wonder what story he created about me, his former student, about why I was standing around in his garage with him on a Saturday, a day when other kids are out with their parents, or watching television, or playing soccer. I imagined a little pity party of him and his girlfriend. Meanwhile, Jeff's hands still had my scent on them, my cigarettes left behind on his coffee table.

I realized my words were something he was not entirely interested in hearing.

"Oh, Wendy," he finally said. "I just see this wall between us, and I wish you would talk to me."

I sighed and rolled my eyes. I pulled the receiver away from my ear for a moment and noticed it was due for a cleaning. I thought of the pungent smell of rubbing alcohol and the security of a small, white cloth. I switched the receiver to my other ear.

"I care about you. A lot. I know you may find it hard to believe, but it's true."

I held the plastic receiver away from my face for a moment, wondering if I should continue listening. I brought it back to my ear and sighed heavily again, exasperated.

There was a marked shift in his voice.

"But I have to tell you, she'll be living in town for a while, and we're going to try to make it work. So you need to know, my energies will be focused elsewhere."

Energies will be focused elsewhere.

My stomach went from warm to ice cold. My hips felt like a jaw slowly closing. My forehead tensed and my face began to tremble. I knew I would not eat the rest of the day.

Later, he told me about how his girlfriend had been cleaning his house and how she put the photograph of me back up on his mantel. How she remarked on my presence.

"She seemed so troubled that day," she had said. "But she still had a *look* about her." Then she returned to dusting.

Hearing this, one part of me laughed and laughed.

His girlfriend, me, him: a sick triangle that she wasn't completely aware of.

Another part of me slept all weekend, dreamt the slow, ocean dreams that came from several tiny blue sleeping pills.

FALL
1987

Football games, freshman dances, and Mass.

In the mornings I pulled on my skirt (gray wool or sky blue cotton), buttoned up my blouse (white or sky blue) and scrunched my socks down on my ankles. I slipped my penny loafers on and turned off the radio. Grabbing my bag, I headed out the door, glancing at the window across the street. The curtains were closed, but the light over the easel glowed.

I stepped over every buckle in the sidewalk, and walked past the house with the assortment of cacti in the front yard, the yellowed lawns, the electrical towers, and the sight of the Hollywood Freeway. It might be a shortened day to accommodate a special afternoon Mass, replete with incense and the hum of incantations; a half-day so the teachers could have an educational retreat; or a full day with the prospect of a dance held in the school's gymnasium at night.

I went to four dances in my four years of high school. The first two were in freshman year.

I went, stood uncomfortably in lines to get pictures taken with my friends, all of us dateless, or I danced with abandon, hoping to catch the eye of Dennis Monroe or any other cute boy who knew that women were multi-orgasmic.

I took early buses home. I opened my journal and refreshed my memory.

My lover was a twenty-nine-year-old man. He had a knee injury. He had shoulder aches and caught colds often. He was a sports fan, not a player, and his body was beginning to show it. He got winded during sex and sometimes couldn't reach orgasm.

When I felt especially academic, I opened up my pile of overdue library books or I turned on the television and tried to concentrate on the cable news broadcast. I found myself staring past the talking heads into the scenes behind them, the whirring computers and people walking back and forth, holding papers and talking into headsets. I opened my journal and considered the finer points of socialism, a topic I looked up in my encyclopedia set. I took notes in thin blue ink, messy, touching the tops and bottoms of the college-ruled lines in a special notebook for such matters.

I pondered with curiosity and subdued anger the arguments made by people on the Donahue show that said music lyrics, movies, and television were too sexually explicit or violent, made by people who could not possibly be referred to as artists. I considered my pot pipe, hidden in its drawer, my friends and their lost virginity, and my desires that had me running back and forth from bus stops in weather hot and cold, ready, waiting for the next sexual encounter that I imagined spoke of love.

One day I was walking home from the bus stop, books balanced in one arm, book bag on my shoulder. I pranced down the familiar street in my uniform that hung loosely on my body, aside from the tucked-in blouse.

A truck driving towards me suddenly stopped, pulling up next to me. A man was in the driver's seat. The huge, elevated tires of the truck gave him an inflated presence, and I looked up, squinting in the sun, expectant of his question. It wasn't unusual for people to get lost in our maze of houses by the freeway.

Instead of rolling down his window, the man opened the driver-side door. He turned his body, lengthened and tan, and exposed himself to me: shiny naked skin, muscle, and hair. He jumped back into his seat, slammed the door, put the truck into gear and sped away.

I stood there for a moment.

I searched my head for a proper response.

Finally I looked around to see if anyone had been looking out their windows. It was hot and sunny, curtains were drawn, driveways were absent of cars. I switched my book bag to my other shoulder and resumed my walk home.

As I stood in front of my screen door, I decided the thing to do would be to tell my mother. She was sober, just home from work. She listened to me, and then sat down at the kitchen phone. I heard her fanning herself in frustration as she indignantly reported this act to the police. I parked myself in the living room where I could listen to her conversation and watched my reflection in the mirrored wall, trying to hold back laughter.

NOTES ON AN EXCAVATION:

TOOLS, 2012

There are materials and equipment required for excavation. These things I learn from my toddler's books.

Curious George visits an archaeological dig and before he upends everything in sight, notices a pick-axe, brushes. Shovels.

My toddler and I learn about the bulldozer, backhoe, grader and excavator. Names of things that move earth around.

First holes, then a foundation. The teeth of the excavator chomp on dirt. Excavation begins and at first glance it is a sign of progress. And yet there is a dismantling that must occur first—perhaps a demolition of buildings that came before, then a cut in the earth, an opening, then the dig.

"No bones here," the archaeologist says in the Curious George book as she sifts through dirt. What looks like bone might just be rock. She is looking for clues. There is a timestamp sealed in the bone's marrow. The bone is a puzzle piece. The bone is a treasure, if only it can be found before "progress" arrives and buildings go up over it, burying it forever.

Opening up my old journals feels like a dig. I wet a finger with my tongue and turn the pages.

NOTES ON AN EXCAVATION:

FAMILY, 1987

Though not divorced yet, my father was mostly living elsewhere. My mother and I lived among each other, having the necessary conversations people who live together have, people with full-time lives and open weekends. One of us split, the other stayed in the house. Both of us used whatever potions we had at hand to make us forget a difficult existence until Monday, when we re-entered the world that seemed normal, the world that might not have forgiven us had it known the oblivion we stepped into each weekend.

My grandmother was a pleading voice on the phone, a plaintive tone of worry. I grew to understand that she helped create the mother I lived with, the one who told me dark, cautionary tales spackled together from news stories she read or heard about, stories she hoped would scare me into being a "good girl."

These were the words I grew up hearing: "Have you been a good girl?"

These are the words my mother says to my own daughter even today. At two, my daughter simply says yes. I wonder what makes a good girl at the age of two. I wonder how we will define, or redefine, what "good girl" means as she gets older because I know my mother will never stop asking.

As I write of my mother and my grandmother, I can't help but think that I wasn't a good girl.

I ran wild. I unleashed rage as often as I could, within boundaries I created in my head, stopping short of physical violence with my mother at least twice. These are instances she would never remember—she was drunk, and one of the times, I was keenly, sharply sober. I wanted to push her away and hoped she felt the push. When she was sober, I wanted her contrition and I wanted to pull her in closer. Closer still.

My mother was yet another adult with whom I was wrestling for power. As the adult, she had power but she relinquished it with the vodka pour and ice clink. I grabbed what tendrils of power I could, tried to completely render her powerless. I didn't yet know the potency, the intensity of mother-power. I thought I saw glimmers of it in the threads that bound my grandmother and mother—the daily phone calls my mother insisted on making to my grandmother though the conversations might be short, sharp, ending in arguments. The pull towards my mother was and is profound, enough that as a teen I tried to pull with all my might in the opposite direction. Not a good girl.

Even now, faced with telling a story in which my mother plays a role, I find myself protective, hurrying to excuse her behavior: she did the best she could. And it's true; she did. That doesn't mean I didn't want to claw my way out of her house. It means I stuck by her, lived with her, did not emancipate myself legally. I made sure she was breathing as she lay passed out before I stole money from her wallet and left the house on an adventure; I continued getting decent grades and behaving with a modicum of decency when she was sober. But I felt I could never be the good girl she or my grandmother had hoped for.

Meanwhile, in the background, my father appeared in and out of my consciousness, an occasional apparition I snuffed out of my head. I could easily imagine his disbelief, his possible anger and disappointment with me had he known my truths. I could easily lie or omit information to my mother and grandmother. I felt lucky I didn't have to also do so with my father. He did not ask me questions about anything other than school when I saw him. Our relationship was based on quiet drives and an understanding that we might not understand one another. Music filled in the silence in the car.

The adults in my life had the power: my parents, Jeff. The girl I was—good, bad, neither or both, saw the discrete openings, the loopholes I could manipulate, and did what she could with them. It was the best I could do.

1988

JANUARY
1988

Hollywood.

Movie theaters seemed to have a more magical quality than in the Valley, where I'm from. Plus the sidewalks glittered.

My friends and I ambled around Hollywood on the weekend nights I talked my mother into letting me leave the house. Before stepping foot outside the door, my fingers clandestinely pulled the plug on the kitchen telephone. After doing the same to my bedroom phone, *click*, we were *off*.

There were carnivals visiting town; the Cinerama Dome Theater, round and impressive; weird, spacey-looking people walking the streets; long-haired men that softly accosted us as our shoes hit the concrete in synchronization: Grass. *Weed. Acid, the best.*

We stepped into a smoky diner and sat in a booth. A man called Alley Cat approached us. Veronica introduced him, and I remembered the pamphlets he gave her of drawings and typewritten manifestos, with the self-titled "Alley Cat" on the front. After coffee mugs were replenished and chugged, Alley Cat led us to his one-bedroom apartment on Cosmo Street.

A fluorescent bulb lit up one end of the room, and the walls were covered in strange posters and drawings I was too shy to look directly at. An electric hum sealed us off from the street. Aquariums lined the room, holding various animals: a pigeon, a cat, a rattlesnake, iguanas, a tarantula. As Alley Cat spoke to us in his gravelly tone, I snuck looks at Veronica and Abigail's faces. Is this real? Is this normal? My body felt tense, preparing to run if need be. The glow of the bulbs made my skin feel itchy.

I was awash in relief when we finally stood up to go. Alley Cat handed us another of his photocopied zines, and we hit Cosmo Street, a faint smell of sewer air hitting my nostrils. We headed back to our friend's car.

Back in the Valley, we smoked cigarettes and drank cup after cup of bitter, wretched coffee served by Carlos, our waiter with whom we all proclaimed we were crushed out on. The circular booth, with electrical tape patching up rips in its beige vinyl, felt secure, warm and peaceful. Abigail laughed as she lit up a cigarette, and I wished I could spend every night this way, embraced by a smooth diner booth, drinking coffee and talking for hours with these brilliant, beautiful people.

I explained this to Jeff after I came home and plugged in my bedroom phone. My mother was crashed on the living room sofa. I wrapped myself up in blankets on my bed, whispering to Jeff about what I wanted, what I wished.

∿

"Yeah, so it's over. Fara and I."

Silence. His voice was cracked with bronchitis, his nose stuffy and he was telling me what I considered the best news of my life.

"Yeah, well, we'll see," I said, urging a sympathetic tone in my voice.

"Yeah, well, would you believe me if I said I don't care if I live or die, I feel so bad?" He coughed and spit phlegm.

My index finger touched the clear surface of the button that could hang up on him. I ran my finger gently over it, imagining a response if I were to push it, hearing a dial tone in place of his voice.

I didn't have to push the button. We hung up soon after. I got up and went to the kitchen, where I fixed myself a Lipton's Cup of Soup in the microwave. I looked out the window to the next door neighbor's house as the microwave whirred. The lights were on, the curtains closed. I wonder if they ever heard my mother and I yelling, the smash of a glass I had thrown out of range of her body so neither of us would get hurt, my point made painlessly. My chest felt heavy, like a storm was going to break inside me. The curtain moved next door. I looked away, down at the yellow Formica and the paper towels with their homey blue flower print. I touched my throat, swallowed and headed back to my bedroom, slamming the door.

~

At Moby Disc, I bought the records *Are You Experienced?* and *Janis Joplin's Greatest Hits.*

I decided I was officially crushed out on Dennis Monroe, the senior from my speech class. I made a big commotion with my friends when I asked him to the Valentine's Dance and an even bigger commotion when he said yes.

"Realistically, Wendy, I hope I'm at least second on your list," Jeff said after we made out passionately that weekend. We were hidden behind the front door, waiting for his roommates to get back from picking up some beer.

"Realistically? What do you mean?" I asked, pulling myself back to look at his face.

"After your beloved Dennis Monroe," he said, bringing me close for another kiss. "Just wait," he said when we came up for air. "We'll laugh about all of this when we're older." Kiss. "That is, if I'm not married and you're not fully attached to that Monroe guy."

Jeff got his way: Dennis broke our date for the dance.

I slumped in my chair in speech class and decided not to turn in his direction anymore, even after he apologized, kindly, appropriately apologetic.

"His loss," Jeff said, and proceeded to outline a new fantasy, one in which I was fucking both of his housemates while he watched.

I held the phone to my ear, curious, silent, listening.

~

Holidays seemed meaningful to Jeff. I received unexpected phone calls and a tone that spoke of deeper things, beyond lust, things that were hard to come by in our regular conversations that increasingly nosedived into silly, petty arguments.

Holidays in my household felt staged. We celebrated the usual ones, like Thanksgiving and Christmas, but my mother had long ago abandoned Easter or Valentine's Day.

"It's that time of year when you tell the women," Jeff said, chuckling, "or, the woman, in your life how you feel about them." I felt acutely aware I was not going to any high school dance.

"Okay," I said, wondering if this conversation was in service to his dick.

"Wendy," he began, "you are one in a million."

"Cliché," I countered.

"Ooh! You're tough," he said. "Okay, okay." I heard the sound of water roiling, the suck of air, the exhale of breath. When he finished taking a hit from the bong, he said slyly, "Will you...run away to Montana with me when you're eighteen and have my children?"

We laughed, although all my muscles clenched in surprise and disbelief.

"You don't know it yet, but you are all mine," he said after describing scenarios involving marriage, children.

I closed my eyes and considered my most secret thoughts, never brought out to see daylight: the fantasies of having children, living in a house with wood floors, lots of plants, and maybe even Jeff. I imagined small children whose hands I held in my own, their hazel eyes gazing up at me, their black curly hair pulled back in a rubber band. I opened my eyes and looked down at my hands: soft, lined, empty.

I thought of these words, the steady stream of love-talk Jeff could initiate, that failed to emerge in our usual interactions. In one instance, he arrived at my door on his motorcycle. I gratefully let him into the house. I was on spring break from school, my mother at work.

When he pushed past me into the living room, refusing to take off his helmet, I leaned against the open door in disgust. I watched him move from room to room, panicky and strange, and wondered how serious this man was about futures involving marriage, children, and me. At the moment he resembled a terrible coke fiend, unable to kiss me because he wanted to keep his helmet on, he was leaving that quickly. I let him pinch and grope my skin with mild interest until he left, roaring away on his motorcycle that made the curtains across the street open.

After I locked the screen door, I went to my room and put on a Pink Floyd tape. I lay face down on the yellow carpet, angered but wanting, and rubbed myself to a soaring, bitter climax.

SPRING
1988

Random days off from school, weekends I could steal away from home and say I was at Abigail's, I spent with Nicholas.

Nicholas wore black t-shirts, cut off at the sleeves, emblazoned with names of heavy metal bands. His curly blond hair was a little longer than I preferred. He was seventeen.

Nicholas's needs seemed as great as mine. Dramatic tendencies were injected into each encounter: slow unbuttoning of my blouse; the pulling off of my panties taking several long, delicious minutes, my hands eager, unbuttoning his Levis, then pausing, pulling back to stretch the time out long, long, longer. We never bothered with sheets or blankets, and rarely with condoms.

Our clothes lay strewn on his bedroom floor until we heard his little sister moving around in the house, home from school. We emerged from his room, satiated. We turned on the television to a talk show, the traffic going by on Roscoe. After a plate of cookies and glasses of milk, we retreated to his room to smoke a pipe load and kiss goodbye.

The bus stop was conveniently located a few yards from his door, and I hummed happily as I waited for my bus home, imagining the details I would include in my next journal entry.

"Jeff, it was the best sex of my life," I squealed into the receiver. I felt full of Nicholas, my clothes ripe with his scent, the smell of skateboards, clean cotton t-shirts and pot. My bare feet danced on the carpet.

"The best, huh? But was it the kinkiest?"

I paused, uncertain. "Kinky" had no clear definition in my mind. Even the word itself seemed extraneous, unnatural. I flashed on the last time Jeff and I were together: my reflection in his mirror. Or the time we used the shoulder massager, does that count?

"You better not get into any trouble," he admonished, breaking my concentration. "Don't get in trouble, get pregnant or anything."

I laughed. My mom was in the living room and I could hear the television blaring. A sitcom took up the air, canned laughter heading down the hallway. I lit up a cigarette and used the lit match to relight a roach in my ashtray and a stick of incense. The door was wide open and Jeff was lecturing me on the phone.

I took a stiff inhale of the joint and waved the lit cigarette in the air.

"I won't," I said finally.

≈

Abigail had introduced me to Nicholas on a cool late winter night in a friend's garage. After a few wine coolers and some shy conversation, we walked to his house, our hands desperate on each other, eventually unlocking the front door of his parent's house. We entered his bedroom, turned out the light, and something shifted internally. A new chapter began. I left off writing in my journal for a month. When I returned, opening its expectant, empty pages, I felt an altogether new kind of alive.

Years later, I think on it as a splendid fluke, another bad joke. Jeff broke up with his girlfriend. And me?

Enter, official boyfriend of my life, number one! You are a high school dropout, and occupational school hopeful! You are just three short years older than me, and three inches taller! You are speckled blue eyes and curly blonde hair! You go on to become the new proto-type for what I find attractive in the boy species! You are freckled and red-bearded and a heavy metal dude-turned-punk rocker! You enjoy smoking too much pot, drinking a whole lot of beer in your friend's garage and haven't had a whole lot of luck with the ladies in a while, which is where I come in! I am not quite fifteen when we meet, which freaks you out a little, but not when we are walking down the street to your house, wasted from rushing through several clumsy wine coolers, kissing under streetlights. You are sweet, boyfriend number one, and much nicer than the punks you hang out with! You are about to embark on a four and a half year relationship with me, in which I will be yours, and others', and yours again, like a loose light switch. You are about to embark with me on an attempt at normalcy, puppy love, and teenage passion. Thanks for participating wholeheartedly, even if you were drunk or stoned a lot, number one! Thanks for playing, boyfriend number one!

～

I could not imagine turning fifteen could be any better than this.

My mother left weekend evenings to go to parties with people I didn't know. I didn't ask questions.

I moved around the house, opened the curtains wide, pulled up blinds, opened windows and bolted the front door.

My hands sorted through the growing stack of records until I found Cream, or Led Zeppelin, and the house began to pulse with sound. After a few phone calls, my friend Danny arrived with Veronica in tow, sometimes with videos to watch: *Altered States*, or cult classics like *The Trip*. We played haphazard games of Quarters with my small stash of wine coolers and Danny's baggie of weed, creating elaborate rules designed to get us completely drunk and high within an hour.

I listened to strangers speak of orange sunshine acid while they passed joints to me and Abigail in the darkness at a Pink Floyd concert. I put lubricated, ribbed, or colored condoms on the flat white counter of the drugstore at the mall along with my money, and no one blinked an eye. I hoisted my backpack over my shoulder, colorful patches multiplying on its canvas. I looked forward to the vodka I confiscated from my mother's bottle. I snorted miniscule amounts of cocaine with a crisply rolled dollar bill off the smooth, pink surface of Abigail's thumbnail. Veronica rolled perfect joints in the bathroom of Chuck E. Cheese's and handed me ten tokens so I could waste time until her shift was over. We went to parties with her group of friends, punks and skinheads, and the whirlwind of parties regularly attended by the LAPD began for me. After the first couple of times, I grew to expect them, their black uniforms approaching on the lawns of houses in neighborhoods I was not familiar with. Hiding in strange bedrooms or bathrooms in complete darkness and silence became a common occurrence; that, or dispersing, my legs moving underneath me, following Veronica, as we ambled down sidewalks in search of the closest bus stop or a friendly driver that might offer us a ride elsewhere.

I used my allowance to buy tickets to an all-day reggae show at the Greek Theater in Los Feliz, where I bought my first water pipe, my first hippie poncho. An hour after we stumbled into the amphitheater, a woman walked onto the stage and announced that we needed to evacuate, that a fire was threatening the nearby mountains.

"This a joke?" I slurred at Veronica.

After some indignant yelling of obscenities and general contempt for the fire and the loss of our tickets, we walked down the stone steps sober-like, trying to give meaning to the term "evacuation."

After some Frisbee on the grass while waiting for the slow line of cars to begin the descent down the hill into Los Feliz, we went to Ben Franks for coffee to sober up a little. After Ben Franks, we rode the freeway to the Valley. We were dropped off at Nicholas's house. He and I might have been on the skids, due to the rumors I was hearing about him seeing other girls, but his house was somewhere to go.

I called out a greeting to his parents in the living room, who waved in response, and opened the door to Nicholas's bedroom. He was playing drunken host to many of his similarly drunken friends in the cramped quarters of his bedroom. We joined the game of Uno already in progress.

∼

"Why are you leaving? You were here all afternoon!" Jeff cried one day as I picked up my backpack and put my shoes on.

Because I'm getting smarter, I thought to myself.

It was not fair for him to have an orgasm, and then beg paranoia to have us stop what we're doing, me orgasmless. I threw out a couple of phrases, beginning with "frustrated" and "pissed off" and he kept repeating the reasons he couldn't get me off, ending with "Why won't you look me in the eye?"

I started on the long walk down to the bus stop, checking my pocket for quarters that might connect me to someone on the restaurant pay phone. Jeff followed. His Siamese cat on her fast-moving, coffee-colored legs followed him close behind.

"Hey!" he yelled as I continued past the halfway mark towards Van Nuys Boulevard, stopping he and his cat in their tracks. "Hey! Are you going to see that movie we talked about tonight? Will you call me and let me know if it's any good? Or call me tomorrow! Hey! We can always say that I owe you one! Don't be mad! C'mon, Wendy!"

Owe you one, my ass, I thought, not bothering to turn around. I kept walking.

∼

I wrote about every sexual encounter in the pages of my journal. Canoga Park is where I often slipped off my shirt at night, with Nicholas's hands reminding me that I was attractive, worthy of kisses after we stole away from his friends so we could be alone against the rocks, dust rising in the air, resting on our jeans.

When I wrote of my body it often seemed like a separate entity I was watching, like there was only partial ownership involved in my own skin. *My* back may have been jammed up against large, graffiti-covered reddish rocks, *my* thighs positioned to cradle the pelvis of a boy with the same intent as me, but it was like I was watching from a few feet away as a girl let her hands caress a boy's neck as he unbuttoned her pants and helped her lift her shirt off in the moonlight.

And even without ownership, there was an awareness—like the stars we can't discern because of the streetlights, although we know they're there—of beauty. Mirrors lie, as do men, but intuitively, I looked down and saw a body, my body, and I liked what I saw. My skin saw the sunlight more. I saw the veins through the hairless, pale parts of my skin; I had emerged from showers, dripping, my steamy image in the mirror something of daydreams. But there it was, reality, as my fingers touched the glass, rubbing until the image came up clear and different from the fourteen-year-old I had seen not that long ago.

Glasses fell by the wayside. I tried contact lenses, beginning with hazel that really appeared yellow, graduating to clear so that my brown eyes showed through, then forays into hair bleach, black dyes, until I knew my real shade of dark brown was the most attractive decision. These changes didn't fall perfect like dominoes in formation, but came into play like mistakes I had to sort through and rethink.

Beauty would never be a static place for me, but it would become more of a belief, a train of thought I rode more consciously, purposefully. Sometimes I only found it in late-night trysts in public parks, or cars, or bedrooms; anywhere my clothes might find a temporary place to land so that my body could be free, seen, explored, enjoyed by myself and others.

∼

One afternoon I met a British man down the street from Chuck E. Cheese's. I clearly saw the ploy, the devices he used cunningly. Bus stops between places, I was most vulnerable. He kept at me to go get a drink with him, when instead I was really on this errand to take the bus home (safe), get some new clothes (smart), then ride the bus back to meet Veronica when she got off work so we could get some pot (Danger. Jackpot.) The word *instead* rang between each thought.

Instead, I chose to let this man buy me drinks, because I knew that with him, no one would card me. My wine coolers came in heavy pint glasses with thick, curvy handles. Sauced, pretending I was twenty-two (and trying to remember I *have* to be twenty-two), he began asking me if I was "daring." I felt my lips curve into a smile.

He unbuttoned the top of my denim shirt in the middle of the empty restaurant. I stumbled to the bathroom, almost puking, and re-buttoned my shirt. I returned and slurred that I needed some air. He suddenly offered that his apartment was nearby, and on the street, he put his lips on mine.

"I have to meet my friend. She's getting off work soon," my mouth said. I wondered how I would explain being wasted at three o'clock in the afternoon to Veronica. I looked forward to the laughter and the ride back to her parent's house, where I could chill out on her bed and watch her smoke cigarette after cigarette in her room. Safe.

Instead, this man followed me to Chuck E. Cheese's. I had birthday parties at Chuck E. Cheese's. I was leading him to a place where children played, where Veronica would be getting off her shift any minute. I couldn't believe he was following me. When he cornered me in a small doorway off the street and started unbuttoning my shirt, I knew I did not want a man with gray hair pushing himself on me in the street. He flicked my nipples through the denim and told me I was beautiful.

"Would you go to my place with me?" he asked. "I want to put it in you."

When I shook my head, staving off nausea, he started pulling money out of his billfold. I saw at least one one-hundred dollar bill.

Years later, I think of the moment when my eyes caught the image of this one-hundred dollar bill, the way it had been folded, then unfolded, and held out to me. It became something to think about intermittently, when I felt suffocated in my room at my mother's house, her voice slicing into me and the scent of vodka permeating my door. The fold, unfold, offer up: when I was telling Jeff on the phone of the previous weekend's exploits. The fold, unfold, offer up: later, when I was a college student, counting out change for the bus to go to school to pick up my student loan check.

Instead, I left the man on the sidewalk and stumbled to Chuck E. Cheese's, where Veronica and Abigail were standing in their red work shirts and red visors, asking, "Who the hell was that!"

"Instead" was the operative word of fourteen, fifteen.

～

One afternoon I walked into Jeff's house. Jeff and Jesse sat at the dining room table talking. I pulled out a seat and sat down with a sigh after a few moments of standing awkwardly in the living room, wishing for an invitation. I slipped off my sandals and let my feet touch the carpet.

"So," Jeff began, looking at the glass tabletop, "how's Bus Stop Wendy?"

"Fine," I said, looking from his face to Jesse's. Jesse smiled broadly at me. We met on one of the numerous Saturdays I happened by, records in hand, wishes blooming in my chest.

I looked at my lap. "But I didn't ride the bus here," I said, picking up my bag and looking inside for a lighter or some matches. "I hitched."

Jeff looked at the table, sighed sharply, stood up. Jesse watched him and then looked at me and shrugged. I could tell Jesse was attracted to me. He made it obvious. I looked away nervously.

"I'm going to explain this once, and once only." Jeff left the room and returned with two pairs of knee-high stockings. I made a face when I saw them, my lip curled, because I was reminded of my mother's wardrobe, the drawer that held such strange items as knee-highs and pantyhose, tan, limp pieces of fine mesh.

"Why do you have those?" I finally laughed, finding my voice, and I looked at Jesse.

"Yeah, man, what are you *doing* with those ugly things?" Jesse asked.

"Wendy, sit back in that chair." I looked up at him and tried not to laugh. I settled deeper into the chair and he used a hand to push my chest back, straight, flush with the chair back.

"So. Let's say you're out there in the world, and you're hitchhiking." Jeff talked in a singsong voice I immediately didn't like. I stared at him as he lengthened one knee-high stocking in his hands and threw the other three on the table.

"And some guy picks you up and you tell him where you wanna go, but he takes you somewhere else. Someplace you haven't been, and don't want to be." Jeff began tying one of my ankles to the chair leg with the hosiery. "Too tight?" he asked, looking up at me. He pushed his glasses up on his nose, his breath coming out in short, hot grunts I felt on my skin.

"A little," I answered, my eyes wide, trying to form a casual smile that wouldn't quite come.

"Good." He took the second stocking off the table and tied my other ankle to the chair. "If it were someone else, they might use rope. Or electrical tape. Or a cord."

"What the fuck, Jeff," I finally stammered as he bent one of my arms back and tied it behind me to the metal arm of the chair. I couldn't look at Jesse; this suddenly felt private and insane, a flaw in Jeff's composition, something I had always wondered about, but could never put my finger on.

When both of my arms and legs were tied to the chair, my chest artificially jutting out, I said again, weakly, "What the fuck."

"Oh, wait, one more thing." Jeff scurried to his bedroom and returned with a bandanna.

"I get it, already," I began, resting my eyes on Jesse. He sat there watching, his brown arms folded across his chest, shaking his head, a slight smile playing on his lips. He couldn't look me in the eye anymore.

"Jeff, man, she gets the picture," Jesse said, taking his eyes off my tied ankles for a moment. Jeff raised one finger at him. He turned back to me.

"Okay, Wendy. You hitchhike, and this is but one possible fate. Do you know there are people out there who will do this to you and any other girl that's out on the street looking to get from one place to another? I mean, how can I make you understand? Look, I have a fucking hard-on here," he said, smacking his crotch through his pants with an open palm.

I didn't look at his crotch. I looked down at the smoke-scented bandanna on my mouth and felt sleepy. My nostrils flared like they do right before I start crying.

"You don't want to get raped. You don't want someone to do this to you. But when you get into their car, you don't know who you're fuckin' dealing with. Some asshole, maybe? You'll never know." He paused dramatically and stood back to admire his work. He untied the bandanna from around my mouth and I pretended not to gulp the air in relief. He was sweating, nearly panting.

"Tell me, Jesse, did it not turn you on to see a pretty young thing tied up like that?" Jeff said, turning to Jesse matter-of-factly as I shook my arms and legs out, the stockings falling to the carpet like small, shed skins.

"Oh, Jeff, man, she understood, she understood," Jesse replied. He turned to me. "Why are you friends with this guy?" he laughed.

My tongue ran over my lips.

"Can I have some water?" I asked, already hating the demure tone I used.

Jeff moved into the kitchen and got a mug from a cabinet. He let the tap run and filled it. He returned, handing it to me with both of his hands, touching mine as I received it. I drank. My heart slowed, beat faintly in my chest.

"Don't hitchhike to get here, okay? That's all I ask," he said to me after sitting back down in the empty chair. A lock of black hair fell on his broad forehead. He gave me a playful kick under the table. I kicked back, stung, speechless.

"Let's have a smoke, shall we?" he said after a moment.

I licked my lips again, wishing for more water. Soon a joint was being born on the glass tabletop, and all, it seemed, was forgotten.

SUMMER
1988

Jeff wasn't home when I called him. But Jesse answered.

"Hey!" I screeched into the phone. Veronica, who was sitting next to me on the bed applying her make-up, shushed me though I could see she was holding back laughter.

"Guess what?" I said into the receiver in a whisper. Veronica patted my hand and put out her cigarette in the glass ashtray. I looked back at the phone and its keypad looked like a strange, otherworldly instrument I'd never seen before.

"What?" Jesse said, playing along.

"I'm on acid and you get to be my ride today!" I exclaimed. Veronica shook her head at me and moved to pick up her purse.

"Where to?" he called out. This was the answer I was looking for.

Half an hour later, his truck was sitting in idle in front of the house. I waited out front where Veronica had stationed me. She was on her way to get some pot, and I had to busy myself for an hour or two while she went out to score. It was summer and the air was thick with heat and her parents were at work. She feared bringing me along on her errand in my hallucinogenic state, especially after

I chewed a sheet of aluminum foil in my mouth and insisted on taking some with me for the ride. "Like chewing gum," I explained.

I rode around with Jesse, the stereo blaring, both of us singing "Hotel California" at the top of our lungs. I hummed to myself absently and let my finger trace the fabric interior of the truck, mystified. Jeff crossed my mind, but since he hadn't answered the phone, I didn't want to think about him.

Jesse returned me to Veronica's and for the next eight hours Veronica and I laughed a lot, traveled by bus, made charming small talk with my mother, winked at each other behind her back, watched television, made mashed potatoes we couldn't eat, stared at the bubbling cheese pimple on a slice of pizza we microwaved, and before sleep arrived at six a.m., I came down on the floor of the bathroom, trying to bring myself to orgasm, tense, full of strychnine and the speed it brought, silent but for my breathing.

Decision-making became secondary to back-to-back experimentations with acid and Ecstasy. We filled halves of capsules with honey to dilute this strange white powder I read about in my freshman health book under the heading "designer drugs." Our hostess, the friend of the drug dealer, rubbed my open palm with her fingertips and said, *Wendy, you just exude sex*, and I beamed, quite taken with this description, my tongue lazily circling the warm, soft insides of my mouth as the Ecstasy took hold. It deposited me in a world where I could hold my friend's hands, stare into their eyes and tell them how much our friendship meant to me as my feet dug into the carpet with sensual abandon. A week later, we lied to our parents so we could kneel together in a strange house with many other people our age, parents conveniently missing, our mouths open, tongues stretched out in wait for the hit of acid to be deposited, ingested, experienced. *Communion*, we called it, our eyes blazing.

FALL
1988

The smoke in my bedroom wasn't dissipating even with the windows open. I was a little nauseated in the cloudy room. I had the dour taste of Pall Mall nonfilters in my mouth, a pack I chose for the novelty of it. My ashtray was almost overflowing with Camel, Kools, and Marlboro filters. All my friends smoked in my room. The walls were taking on a tannish tint. I knew my mother would make me paint when I moved out, whenever that might be.

I felt a thirst that started in my chest, radiating out to my throat, only I didn't want to go get a diet Coke from the fridge, because it was after ten and my mom still wasn't home, and I had left all the lights off in the living room when I got home from school.

I wore the same cut-off jeans I'd worn for days after school. The errant strings hung off the tattered edges and tickled my knees and the insides of my legs. I smoothed a hand over one leg that was freshly smooth, a little sensitive from the brisk rub of a razor. I poked at the little scabs on my knees that looked like tiny dark islands on my skin.

My white peasant blouse, as light and airy as it was, scratched my raw, pink shoulders. I got sunburnt a couple days before, and parts of my skin had already transformed from pink to a deep brown, but my shoulders still felt tender and hot. My sandals, which laced up onto my calves, felt a little too tight and were rubbing me the wrong way.

I was achy, annoyed. I stood up and pushed the window sideways in its groove until it was up against the small, square piece of metal that served as a lock. It didn't occur to me to run away. The room was an oasis, a still point. Dust wafted toward me and fell like a heavy fog of glitter into the air.

I hope I get my period soon, I thought.

FALL & WINTER 1988

I was moving in the circles of hippie-come-latelies, punks, skinheads for racial unity, and drug addicts. I felt comfortable and chameleon-like among each group, as though each encompassed parts of me that I was still formulating, negotiating.

I was six months from a driver's license. My sights were set on a Volkswagen bus, a thought my parents abhorred, but didn't argue with. I was in negotiations to set free some of the money in the bank account that was not really mine until I turned eighteen. Good grades, decent behavior and refraining from losing my temper all served this purpose. Showing my grandmother good report cards issued from Catholic school, reassuring her that I prayed every time I got into a car and before I went to sleep, that I read my Bible—these worked in my favor. I regularly picked up *Auto Trader* magazine as each new issue hit the stands. I daydreamed of the iconic vehicle that would ensure my status as a hippie girl: the blue bus. I dreamed of the perfect VW that I could adorn with batik fabric on the seats, translucent rainbow stickers I collected from Grateful Dead and reggae shows. I just needed one with an automatic transmission.

I was set on the color blue as a means to achieve a mythical stature I aspired to. *The blue bus, is calling us*, Jim Morrison crooned through my stereo speakers, and I chimed in, trying to echo the crazy, hollow voice, *Driver, where you takin' us?*

A few days before Christmas, Jeff dropped by my house. My mother was safely at work for the next four hours. I was on Christmas vacation, had spent the night before snorting four lines of coke with my new friend, James, who was twenty-one and an alcoholic, and who I was having a hard time finding some redeeming qualities in, besides the fact that he could score me free drugs. I'd met James at the head shop on Van Nuys Boulevard, whose reputation was twenty years old by the time my underaged self wandered nonchalantly onto the premises. James had long, feathered hair and a big, white Buick, both of which bewitched me to some degree, and we easily became friends.

I was at home, my body feeling a little edgy from the night before, and here came Jeff—a surprise visit, totally abnormal, considering his low-grade paranoia—and I was not prepared in any special way. I wore my green, blue and white speckled tie-dye shirt and torn jeans. On my feet were mint green slippers that belonged to my mom, a tiny pink satin rosebud adorning the top of each slipper. In a little while, James was supposed to pick me up, and I was hoping for sooner rather than later, because my mom wanted me home when she pulled in from her day at work.

Jeff came to my door in a scratchy flannel shirt, blue sweatpants and a blue baseball cap. His hair looked longer and he had a thick beard, like he'd been without a shave for a couple of weeks. I realized it had been awhile since I'd seen him.

"Can I use your bathroom?" he asked me as I opened the door. He was chewing tobacco. I nodded with a secret smile.

I was so glad he was there.

Then I remembered the potential awkwardness of James, his constant insecurity and uncertainty. I remembered that he might arrive any minute.

I heard Jeff turning on the sink and I closed and locked the front door. By the time he was done in the bathroom, I was in my bedroom, placing *Led Zeppelin III* on the stereo. He found me carefully putting needle to vinyl.

"Yeah, so your Christmas present's in the car. I'll go get it in a second, but do you wanna get high first?"

"Yeah!" I replied, when really I was thinking *Fuck, yeah!* He produced a strange little pipe in a cute case and some herb that looked as electric green as my tie-dye shirt. We returned to the living room, where he loaded the pipe and handed it over to me. I took a long drag and handed it back. He took a hit that far surpassed mine in inhalation and amount of smoke expelled. I took one more hit and I was *done*, just flying. We were chatty, both of us, and I was stepping on his toes in my green slippers, giggling, aware of how stupid I must look. After a bit, he deserted me, unlocking the front door and stepping outside to retrieve my gift. I looked out at him through the screen door and noticed that he arrived in his roommate's truck. He returned, bearing packages.

Wrapped in the comic pages of the *L.A. Times*, I found two new car floor mats emblazoned VOLKSWAGEN. The second package contained a blue and white license plate stamped with the VW insignia.

I dropped both onto the couch and commenced to laughing, covering my face, and he joined me in laughter, saying over and over, "You like it? Isn't it great? Is it perfect, or what?" The smell of rubber was on my fingers, which were black with newspaper ink. I finally thanked him, wanting to hug or kiss him, and we sat there smiling, my stomach muscles aching from the all the laughter and screeching.

"So," he said, and I felt a shift in tone, "let's go over all the different ways people express 'Merry Christmas' to one another. First, there's this." He stood up, pulled me to my feet, and hugged me. It felt strange and I laughed again, because there was warmth and closeness that I didn't know what to do with.

Next he shook my hand. "Merry Christmas," he said formally.

Before I could react, he put his hands on my breasts and squeezed. "Merry X-mas," he said in a sinister tone. I laughed and swatted at him.

"Merry Christmas," he repeated, and leaned over finally to give me a small peck on the lips. My inhibitions were gone, I was high and forgetful and I moved to him, attempting for a longer kiss, the kind I fantasized about.

"I fooled you there," he whispered, and moved closer to me, enveloping me in a long, passionate kiss that I associated with movies, where the focus went blurry and soft. I felt myself smiling as he licked my earlobes, my neck, my face. We stood there in the living room, in front of the wall of mirrors, making out, and I heard him telling me between kisses to never doubt our friendship, ever. I pressed against him, not saying a word, feeling the roughness of his flannel, the soft brush of his beard on my face.

"I understand why men are always after you," he began, rubbing my ass with one of his hands. I was lost in this arousal, unknowing of where he was going with this talk, what men he was even referring to.

"I mean, one: you're mentally stimulating," he said, followed by a nip on my neck. "Two: because you're physically attractive." I reddened and looked down at the green slippers on my feet, and he touched my face, sucked on my earlobe.

"And, three," he rocked me in his arms, looked me in the eye, "you're just physically overwhelming and you fuck like you're ageless." I pulled back and laughed in confusion, loving the sound of this. *Ageless.*

"Anyone can put you in the tenth grade and you'd function, but I know you, your mind is actually screaming *thirty! Thirty!*" His hazel eyes gleamed, and I focused on the gap in his teeth, the fur on his cheeks, his soft, vulnerable chin, his glasses that I wanted to slip off his face.

I felt inclined to reward him for all of this, the gifts, the pot, the beautiful words. He was breathing heavily into my ear and my clothes were coming off. Soon, Led Zeppelin was over, the needle picked up from the vinyl, and we paused for a moment, breathing in the silence.

Rad, I thought, as he lifted off me and I pulled my panties back to their normal position, *I'm still high!*

"Thanks again," I said, "for the presents."

"Oh, my pleasure," he said with a chuckle and a wink, letting a finger trace along the collar of my shirt. "Oh, Wendy, Wendy, Wendy. I can't wait until you're eighteen, when we can go anywhere together," he said. "We can go to the coast. Anywhere." He snapped his fingers. "And no one can do a thing 'cause you'll be legal."

I sighed, smiling. *Don't, don't go, I thought.*

"Please don't ever doubt our friendship again," Jeff said, and I shook my head, shaking off doubts, sadness, anger and jealousy that had been building like plaque over several months of arguments when we saw one another, phone calls that felt stunted and full of what was unsaid.

He left. In a flash I was over him leaving. James was picking me up soon. And I had to be back by four, when my mom got home.

I headed to the shower, singing.

1989

1989

1989 was the year I went on the Pill.

The granddaughter of this revolution, I purchased mine by donation at the local Planned Parenthood. I was blessed with insurance due to my mother's job, but I didn't want her finding out about my new drug of choice from some mislaid insurance paperwork. I rode the bus to the clinic, filled out the appropriate forms, survived my first gynecology exam and walked away with the pink, plastic shells that contained what would become a daily routine that would keep me free of fear and pregnancy.

Jeff and I celebrated the lack of need for condoms without saying so. He walked around the apartment in only his jeans and made me coffee. We sat at the kitchen bar, drinking mugs of the rich goodness, sharing a bongload, talking, laughing. If this is how life will be with us in the future, I'll take its comfort, laughter, and closeness, I later wrote in my journal, examining the feeling from every angle as we talked and looked into each other's eyes.

One afternoon, I was walking through the sunset-lit aisles of cars in the parking lot of The Forum in Inglewood, waiting for the Grateful Dead to go onstage. I bought six hits of acid and twenty dollars' worth of Ecstasy. I followed my friends as we searched for a big, red bus that purportedly held countless canisters of nitrous oxide. When we found it, we sat on the cement, yelping and shrieking in between inhalations of laughing gas. My hair was tied haphazardly in a rubber band, and wisps of it tickled my cheeks. The evening felt equally full with abandon and promise.

I heard a man whining nearby, pining away for just one dose of LSD, just one. I followed the sound and came to a skinny dude sitting on an open tailgate of a pick-up truck.

I wanted him to experience the beauty, the potential that was me, that was this day, and I wanted my fingers to be gold. I decided to be the fairy, the princess, the one who would save him.

I gave him the tiny piece of paper that I wished would be the best trip of his life.

"Stick out your tongue," I said, and he obeyed; I placed the square paper on his tongue and walked away, floating, an imaginary trail of golden, sexual, generous power emanating from my body as I receded down the crowded aisles.

~

I wasn't the only one changing.

I tried to see the sunny side of my mother's new wardrobe, her laughing demeanor, and saucy asides that let me know she was a woman, with needs and desires like anyone else.

There was the fact that she went out at night and left me alone until ten or eleven, when I had to leave all the lights on, because she herself had scared me into doing so. Still, I enjoyed the empty house, the belief that this was what it would be like to live on my own someday.

Her choice of radio station was the one I had abandoned in favor of classic rock stations. This was not a total loss to me: I could often hear Depeche Mode echoing darkly from the living room and listen along with an air of nostalgia for the songs I had listened to three long years before.

She suddenly spoke of friends at work, possible weekend trips, and asked how I'd feel if she joined a busload of her coworkers on a trip to Las Vegas. I kept my excitement in check even as my pulse raced and my mind calculated how many people I would invite, how much money I had to purchase the necessities for the weekend: beer, wine coolers, an eighth of pot, a bit of coke, some acid.

"You can trust me," I said a little too quickly. Her eyes narrowed.

"Really?" she asked. She thought a moment as she stared me down. "You could invite a couple of your friends over, like Veronica, Dawn." She raised an obscenely red painted fingernail to my chest and pointed. "But no boys, do you hear me?"

"Not even just Nicholas?" I pleaded. She had met Nicholas, spoken to him on the phone, and had acknowledged that there was little to fear with such a soft-spoken, polite nineteen-year-old.

"No," she said, pursing her lips.

"Alright," I said with a sigh. "It'll be fine, don't worry." We looked at each other a moment longer.

When she left my bedroom and I heard her far down the hall, I jumped off my bed and did a little dance. I stifled an excited scream. I picked up the phone and start making calls.

∿

A jug of wine. Me in my cut-off overalls with an Indian print shirt underneath.

Smoke rising in the low-lit living room as another knock sounded on the front door and someone scrambled to answer it. Cross-legged on the floor, it was Friday night and they were all here, my friends in their loose, flowing hippie garb, Nicholas and his friends in their t-shirts and jeans and black leather jackets. People lounged on the sofa with ashtrays between them, and I started up a new pipe load. We used the low glass table to snort a couple lines of coke. Two men, one in black sixteen-hole Doc Martens and the other in a white puffy blouse had an angry exchange about peace. I ran to my bedroom where Veronica had crashed and asked her to referee, help me kick someone out. Jimi Hendrix asked us if this is love or is it confusion. Nicholas detoured me when I got up for more wine and we moved into my mother's bedroom. We slipped off our clothes and fucked, our bodies contorting in myriad positions, and from far away I heard the phone ringing. My hurried hands searched for my clothes: there was no phone in the room, and I could only hope that Veronica had answered it. My mother loved and trusted Veronica, almost as much as I did. When I emerged, Veronica was holding the phone out to me, and I answered. My mother asked what took me so long, and I explained I was in the bathroom and Veronica nodded. Fine and good, I said, urging sober reverence into my voice. I covered the mouthpiece so she couldn't hear the din in the living room.

Everyone slept over. When they left the next morning, Veronica drove us to Planned Parenthood to pick up my new packet of birth control pills. We returned to my house and hung out all day, smoking pot, cooking eggs, opening packages of cookies and cans of cola. Three more friends joined us in the afternoon. We had set aside this special afternoon to drop acid.

A photo was snapped of me with two squares of paper on my tongue. When I tried to write, it came out in spirals and squiggles and I got stuck in the middle of sentences, stopping to stare at my hand, the delicate veins in which I could see the blood pumping along. Everyone was watching *Pink Floyd: The Wall* in the living room, my pen was stuck in the confines of two blue lines on this stuff called paper, and Jeff was looming in my frying mind.

I didn't think of the early morning hours, when we would have to clean up the spilled beer, cigarette box wrappers, hide the pot, and air out the house even as we were coming down, our stomachs uneasy with strychnine. I didn't think of the sleep I needed. I didn't think of my friends, my loyal and generous girlfriends, who helped me make the house spotless just hours before my mother was due home. I didn't think of anything but recording the happenings in my journal, later, sober, fresh from experiences and revelations.

~

"Damn it, I didn't know all those people would be here," he whispered into the phone at me.

I had made a stop at his house during my spring break, my mother's car and learner's permit in my possession. "If you're driving around illegal tomorrow, come by my house and get illegal," he said on the phone the night before. The next day, I'd walked into a living room full of men, composed of coaches from my junior high and elementary school, and a few of Jeff's current and previous roommates. The male energy in the room was like the possibility of wild, cracking thunder in an electrical storm, and I left quickly.

"I'd been planning to tie you up and rape you," Jeff continued on the phone with a sensuous drawl in his voice. "Would you have fought back?"

I listened, my eyebrows furrowed. I felt clueless and tired, unsure of innuendo, confused by fantasy and reality. "No," I said quietly.

"Ah, Wendy," Jeff boomed into the phone, like I had ruined a good joke, "you take the fun out of everything!"

~

Every other visit to Jeff's house seemed drenched in unspoken melodrama. His friends made it known that my presence was suspect, while at the same time, desired. Jeff passed on notes they made about my appearance, and there was a hint that everyone wondered just who I was sleeping with.

The word *slut* seemed to be transfixed in the air above my head: Nicholas had already broken up with me once, suggesting my identity as a *slut* as the reason. I listened to stories Jeff told of the sleep-around behavior of his friends. I wondered what made them *not* sluts.

And then there was the matter that sometimes after a loud, raucous session in his bedroom, Jeff would forget to call me. For days.

I applied ice to the reddish violet bruise-kisses on my skin and took the daily pink pill, peach pill, white pill into my mouth to prevent pregnancy. I answered the phone when Nicholas called and stepped out of my house with a secret smile when he arrived in his car to pick me up, the vehicle weighted down with amps, guitars, cords, beer. I slid back easily into teenage girl mode as easily as I slid into Nicholas's car as he tore away from my mother's house.

EARLY JUNE
1989

I imagined I was a woman relaxing by a pool.

Actually, I was a girl, coming down from an afternoon of strawberry and apple Boone's Farm, sitting at the edge of the half-pipe in Nicholas's backyard, watching him skate up and down in a fascinating arc.

I was reading the *L.A. Weekly* when my eyes weren't closed. I felt vulnerable to the Santa Ana winds in my favorite orange flowered breezy sleeveless shirt and my holey-kneed jeans. My sunglasses made me look older, or so I was told.

I was constantly being told, by varying sources, that I could not possibly be sixteen.

According to these sources, I was "ageless" and also "ancient." I took these as compliments. Depending on what their motives were, the sources also used my agelessness to their advantage; the assuaging of their guilt, for instance. I preferred not to think about it too hard and just baked in the sun and focused on the sound of wheels on wood as they arced, receded, got louder again.

~

Lounging on the grass, I imagined I was a model, waiting to be discovered.

I remembered I was not a model when Jeff's eyes scanned other people in the park, reminding us that we needed to be on the lookout.

I was a girl, lying on the fluffy grass of a park in Van Nuys, Jeff next to me. I was almost contorted in my reclining position so that he would see, remember the way my body looked, the way it bent and posed.

That day he was not thinking about sex, though. He was pondering "us."

I found it unnerving that this thirty-one year-old man wanted to wonder whether or not what we have been doing for almost three years was "wrong." All I could think is that "wrong" was just something in quotation marks. I said this, and he sighed, shook his head. I realized that was maybe the sixteen-year-old thing to say. I was often guilty of this.

With my eyes closed, I felt the sun beating down on me. It felt cleansing. I listened to the ice cream truck take its time passing the nearby playground. I remembered the dark places of the stone castle that inhabited a large part of the playground, because this was where we often came for class field trips when I was in elementary school. The upper level of the castle was a maze that smelled like piss. I used to like to linger there, scaring myself and screeching in delight when someone happened by.

I knew that I would no longer be able to go to that play castle. That soon I wouldn't be able to even physically fit into its small entranceways. Jeff took no notice of the deep breath I took. He had no interest in my past. I wondered if I even had any interest in what was past anymore.

I sat up, grasped my arms around my legs, rocked in the sun, let the moment pass.

Jeff and I made small talk that said: *No sex until the guilt is over.* Sitting up, I could already see the way I looked moments before, lying on the grass, posed. Shame snaked out of me, like a stain spreading underneath me onto the innocent grass.

I realized, for a second, that Jeff could not have, never did, "discover" me and my potential as a girl, a woman, a person who could call herself a writer. And he remembered me, my poses and contortions, only when it suited him.

I realized this, for one sun-drenched, tickling grass, Van Nuys second, and then it escaped me.

When I lay back on the grass again, my mother's car keys fell out of my pocket. I heard them fall and instead concentrated on my ability to maintain Jeff's attention.

EARLY SUMMER
1989

My eighth grade class held a class reunion in the summer after my sophomore year of high school.

I relished getting together with this group of students, even though many of them went to my high school, were even in some of my current classes. The party seemed to be an opportunity to show off burgeoning adulthood: many of us would be arriving in cars that we drove, wearing clothes not chosen for us by our parents or our high school, and I myself planned on eating a pot-laced brownie before arriving, for the novelty of it.

The photographs from that evening are like a situational comedy caught on stills.

My face takes up most of the frame in many of the pictures: I am sunburned, and my hair is long, dark and wavy. My mouth is open and I look as though I've never stopped laughing. In various frames, I am standing with Tammy, or Curtis, or Veronica, and I'm holding a prop of some sort and staring at it in mock fascination for effect. The group pictures feature everyone open-mouthed, laughing, someone's two fingers behind another's head, one person looking at someone out of frame in confusion.

Then there is the sole picture of the teachers. Mr. Connell and Mr. Ivers, as we still called them, are seated by the hostess's swimming pool. I trained my mouth ahead of time to form the words again and again: *Mr. Ivers, Mr. Ivers*, I said into the mirror in my bedroom before the party.

Jeff wore black shorts and a white t-shirt that read "Mammoth Times." His baseball cap was askew and his beard was nearly grown in but sloppy, slightly unkempt. In the photo, his outstretched arm is holding a Budweiser and he's grinning. Mr. Connell looks relaxed, leaning into the poolside chair, a can of Coca Cola at his side.

"Mr. Ivers, Mr. Connell?" I had asked. "Can I take your picture?" I let my eyes linger on Jeff's face for a second more before I snapped the photo.

We made plans to meet after the party, at his house, at half past midnight. I pushed away thoughts of my curfew, my mother's wrath should she be awake and sober when I arrived home. "I have a couple of things I want to say," I started. I sat on the loveseat while Jeff sprawled on his couch. The television was on, the lights out, no one else was home, and there was an emptiness in the air that made it hard for me to breathe. He listened in silence.

"I just wonder, all the time, what our relationship means," I said, trying to keep my tone level, adult. "I don't want our friendship to be just about sex, but sometimes I wonder if it is."

There was a moment of silence, and he sighed.

"You just can't keep perspective." His eyes looked closed as he peered at me from his reclined position. The blue light from the television lit the room.

My thighs were pressed together, tense. I knew that if tears fell, it would be too dark for him to see them. I knew, too, that he might not respond. The night had been a blur of laughter that felt contrived, pulled deep from my insides, as I stood around my peers with Jeff somewhere in the background. My ears had been tuned to him, my eyes flashing and glancing around so that I could spot him casually and track his movements. I questioned every nuance of conversation he made with my female friends, and I carried these images in my pocket to inspect later for innuendo I might have missed. The energy to act normal, happy, seemed to come from a well inside me that gushed and roiled until it drained out when it was clear that Jeff was ignoring me. I was confused by what I wanted: his attention at a party? His professed love in private? "Lovemaking" instead of fucking?

He interrupted my thoughts with a cold, flat voice.

"Maybe we shouldn't have sex anymore. I don't want it to be the only thing that holds us together, and you seem to always have some questions around that."

"Yes," I agreed quickly, my eyes filling up with water, my chest feeling hollow.

"We can get together and shoot the shit, whatever, without sex," he continued intoning from the couch. His lips seemed not to move. He looked exhausted in a way I had never witnessed. "Maybe then we'll—no," he paused, "*you'll* be able to decide whether we're still capable of having fun together, being friends."

"Okay," I said. I stood up resolutely and wondered silently if I could still ask for a kiss.

"Bye," I finally said softly. He lifted a hand to me from the couch. I let my keys jingle in my hand as I opened the screen door and let myself out into the night.

≈

The chugging, whirring noises of my bus mimicked what I imagined to be my own internal hum.

This hum was charged with hope, challenged by the experiences that drugs gave (mind-expanders, I believed), the motor fueled by desire that ran underground but kept me alert, wanting.

The bus, however, broke down numerous times from the moment it was purchased off the used car lot, its sticker price washed off the windshield. The summer that stretched out ahead of me seemed to putt-putt into an unexpected ending whenever the engine died.

My exasperation was lifted when Jeff offered to help fix it, and I watched him as he toiled in my mother's garage. I wondered about this new friendship: was it something we were reinvoking, or concocting?

My mother brought out iced soft drinks and watched Jeff as he inspected the engine. After some small talk, which he answered in his signature charming way, she stood in silence. Her patience thin as always, she returned to the house, calling after me to follow her.

In the muggy air of the enclosed patio, she whispered to me urgently.

"Why does he want to help you so much?"

I looked at her thick skin, her red face from being out in the heat of the garage. I stood over her, inches taller, my hands in my back jeans pockets. I shrugged.

"He's a nice person. He's my friend now that he's not my teacher. Lots of students get advice from him, and he's..." I ran out of adjectives.

"Okay," my mom said slowly, enunciating each syllable. Her lips were red with a skinny line of moist lipstick, her forehead perspiring. "Are you planning on offering him money?"

"We'll see," I said by way of answer and moved away from her, back to the garage. I let the patio door slam shut. I sighed with relief and a light went on in my head and disappeared just as fast.

Could she suspect?

When I returned to the garage, Jeff had rolled the bus onto the sloping driveway and pulled the emergency brake.

"I needed more air," he said. "And light." His dirty arm motioned to the sky. The sun was just starting to go down and an electric guitar blared on the radio. An airplane flew overhead. I kneeled down next to him, my bare feet pressed into the rocky blacktop.

"Now you know that I wouldn't just do this for anyone," he grunted as he used a huge wrench inside the guts of the bus.

"Yeah," I said, looking down at the ground.

"That's why," he said between short exhales of breath, twisting the piece of metal, checking his work, "it makes me so—" *twist,* "fucking mad that you would even—" *twist*, "insinuate that we are not friends first and foremost." He backed away from the bus and threw the wrench down on the ground. It landed near my feet and I stepped back.

"I care, Wendy, which is why I come over in the fucking heat on a gorgeous day to help you out with your bus," he said, his hazel eyes fixed on my face. I nodded and looked at my legs. I felt like I couldn't speak, a feeling I was more than used to with Jeff.

"Get me a beer, would you?" he asked, exhaling. I stood up and pulled open the door of my bus and retrieved a can from the paper bag. It was still cold from the trip he had made to Chief Auto Parts and the liquor store.

When Jeff finished his beer, he produced a baggie and we poked a pinhole into the spent beer can with a paperclip I found on the floor of the bus. He sprinkled a thumbnail-sized amount of pot onto the hole and we each took a long, clean hit from the mouth of the can, sinking the ash into the hole.

~

"I have a graduation to go to tonight," Jeff said a few days later.

"Let's see," he checked the clock, "it's noon now, and my housemate has to borrow my car to get to work tonight," he considered aloud.

I waited, rubbed some lingering sweat from my forehead, the sides of my face. I wiped my hand on my cut-off jeans.

"Can you drive me over to this girl's graduation I have going on later?" Jeff asked. His glasses were slipping off his nose, his face shiny in the heat.

"Yeah," I said, eager, my body feeling lighter as he outlined his plan. "Then what?"

"Maybe you could just drive me there and drop me off, wait nearby, then pick me up." He glanced at the clock again. "Let's hit it. I need to figure out where this thing is exactly."

Beverly Hills?" I asked petulantly when he started describing the itinerary. Jeff rushed around the house in slacks and an unbuttoned dress shirt, intermittently stopping to spit the chew from his mouth into the sink. I grimaced.

"Wha'?" Jeff asked when he saw my face. He still had to shave and he couldn't find his socks. I wasn't sure if I was reacting to the chewing tobacco, or to the prospect of Beverly Hills. A seed of fear settled in my stomach, imagining driving around Beverly Hills, where I had never been.

I collapsed dramatically onto the couch. "Oh my god, this is gonna be a long, long drive," I said. "And this heat..."

"Look, do you wanna help me out or not?" Jeff said, pulling on the found socks and his shiny shoes with a grunt.

"Yes," I groaned. This felt like something you do for friends. The arguments, the annoyances, suddenly had less to do with skin or desire and more to do with the everyday, the mundane. I like this, I thought, as I let my sandals slip off my feet.

"Alright then," Jeff said, spitting a brown mess into the sink and turning the faucet on. He buttoned his shirt and disappeared into his bedroom to find a tie. I sighed loudly.

Half an hour later he was maneuvering my bus onto the freeway. The seed of fear gave birth to something new, an anticipation for whatever was going to happen next. As I relaxed into my seat and pushed my blue-tinted sunglasses up on my nose, Jeff cried out.

"Did you bring the directions?"

"No, didn't you?" I said, shooting from my seat, the strap of the seatbelt resisting against me.

"Okay. Forget this. This isn't happening," Jeff said, checking the rearview mirror, looking to get off at the next exit.

"What? You're not going to go now? You got all dressed up for nothing?" His attitude suddenly struck me as ridiculous. "Just go home and get the directions."

"We're totally late already," Jeff moaned. His right eye twitched. A calm came over me.

"Look, will this girl know you're late?" I asked. I imagined an auditorium, faces beaming on a stage as junior high diplomas were handed out. "She probably won't notice," I continued, thinking this would probably end a lot sooner than he thought, and we might be heading back to the Valley before nightfall.

"You're right, you're right," Jeff said. He flipped the turn signal and I settled back into my seat.

We sped back to his house. Directions in hand, we started off again. Jeff talked frantically, chewing away, using an old Gatorade bottle as his spittoon. He told me about Laurie, the student who was graduating, and how she had once been a student of his but transferred out. "She's a fucking genius," he said, his eyes scanning the lanes of the freeway. I took the opportunity to stare at him as he talked, letting him know that I might be slightly suspicious, possibly jealous. His face didn't change.

"She writes poetry and stuff, like you do, but totally not like you at all. But she sort of reminds me of you," he said, taking his eyes off the road to look at me with a kind smile. I looked back at the road, the line of cars in front of us, the brown hills on either side of us.

As we pulled off the freeway into the streets, I looked at the houses in silence. We passed through neighborhoods with coffee shops and outdoor tables with umbrellas on them. People were sitting outside, drinking out of wine glasses or petite demitasse cups with saucers, laughing under the palm trees. I became conscious of my cut-off jeans with patches on them, my tie-dye t-shirt. As Jeff pulled into the parking lot of the junior high school, I sat limply, wondering what I would do while Jeff ventured inside and acted the part of teacher.

"Just come in," Jeff said after he stepped out of the bus. He swished the remaining chew in his mouth out with water from a plastic bottle I kept in the bus and spit onto the asphalt.

I followed him, his legs moving long and fast to enter the hushed auditorium. It felt like a cool, dark cave. We quietly entered and found seats in the back. I relaxed in the darkness, until the ceremony ended. Our legs had been touching, and this had felt centering, even as I felt the uncertainty of what would happen next.

Jeff stood by the doors as the families filtered out into the sunset. When he spotted Laurie and her family, he approached them with congratulations. I stood by until he introduced me as the ex-student who saved his life by getting him there, since he was without a car. "Wonderful!" Laurie's mother exclaimed, taking my arm. Laurie smiled at me and I saw the glimmer of innocence, the openness in her face that told me she and Jeff were, I thought, simply a student, a teacher, nothing more. I breathed a sigh of relief and let Laurie's mother, Barbara, chatter at me about Oakcrest School, the Valley, the summer ahead.

Barbara and Laurie's father, Larry, treated us to dinner at Ed Debevic's. I couldn't help staring at them, their youngish faces, Barbara's platinum blond hair and twinkling eyes, Larry's handsome fatherliness. They joked, laughed and engaged me in conversation. When I retreated to the restroom, Barbara followed.

In the small quarters of the sitting area by the restroom, she lit up a cigarette.

"Want one?" she asked, offering me her pack. I hesitated.

"Really, now, what is there to hide? What's a cigarette between us girls?" she said gently with her perfect lipstick smile.

I took a cigarette, and she reached over to light it for me. We talked about my high school, what classes I was taking, and my bus. I forgot that I had to pee and leaned against the clean white wall of the bathroom, letting my mature side take over, forgetting my tie-dye shirt and patched up jeans, letting Barbara see the side of me I enjoyed sharing with adults.

We said our goodbyes in the parking lot. There was hand-holding and cheers and laughter, and for whatever reason, I felt like I'd been included in a very special way I didn't totally understand. I almost forgot Jeff was there, I was so engaged with Laurie, the poet genius girl, and Barbara, her beautiful and understanding mother.

After I slammed the door of the bus and Jeff turned the ignition, I remembered I had to pee.

"Really?" Jeff asked as we pulled out into traffic. Barbara and Larry's convertible was ahead of us, and Laurie was waving and smiling.

"Yeah, and I need you to stop somewhere so I can buy some cigarettes," I said, waving back at Laurie.

At the first stoplight, Jeff threw open the door and jumped out of the bus. He ran over to the convertible and motioned to me, talking and smiling, and Barbara nodded.

"Follow us!" Barbara turned and called out. Jeff jumped back into the driver's seat as the light turned green and we tailed the convertible through the streets.

Barbara and Larry lived in a condo in Beverly Hills. They poured glasses of champagne, which I made sure to sip daintily. I found myself talking to Larry, who, after ten minutes of happily chatting, was eager for me to meet his younger brother who would be traveling out from New York for the summer.

"He's seventeen, Wendy, and I think you two would really hit it off," he said with unbridled enthusiasm. I nodded, smiling, and said, "Sure. That sounds fun." I noticed Jeff out of the corner of my eye, laughing with Barbara. When I looked, his eyes told me he was listening. I thought I saw encouragement in them until Barbara interrupted by suggesting that she and I take their dog Oliver for a walk.

She picked up the leash, attached their poodle to it, and we headed outside.

"Let's get some cigarettes," she said once we were out the door, her eyes bright. I found myself listening to her voice, answering her questions, enjoying each pause and interjection, the laughter and adult asides she granted me.

When we returned, Larry and Jeff were standing in the kitchen and Laurie looked as though she was ready to fall asleep. Her blond hair fell against her shoulders and her eyes were half-open, a slight smile on her face.

"Excuse us for a second," Larry said, ushering Jeff into another room. "I have some old albums I think Ivers here would be most interested in."

When they returned, I could smell a faint scent of pot smoke and I decided not to mention it when my eyes fell on Laurie, who had since curled up on the couch while Barbara and I talked.

As we prepared to leave with a second round of goodbyes, Barbara scribbled their phone number onto a piece of paper. Larry handed it to me.

"Really, you and Joseph will get along great. He's into meditation, he's a vegetarian, listens to the Grateful Dead. He'll love you!" He laughed and cried out, "He'll propose to you!" I laughed, blushing, wondering what Larry could see that I could not.

"And we'd love to see you again! Do call us," Barbara added.

Next thing I knew, Jeff and I were back on the freeway, eventually pulling up in Jeff's driveway. I moved over to the driver's seat and said goodbye to him absently, my head filled with laughter, the thought of family, and a sense of normalcy that I found strangely exotic, and even appealing.

SUMMER
1989

The heat split the morning in two. It was Sunday. My eyes felt heavy from sleep, sweat already forming on my upper lip before ten a.m. I had a special date with Jeff, and I was not afraid to think date as I leaned toward the mirror in my bra and panties and applied a little gloss to my lips, which looked to me, smooth, sexy, worthy of kisses.

I pulled on my new favorite dress, one that testified to the coke, sleeping pills, and cigarettes I'd been ingesting pretty regularly. It was teeny-tiny short, and clung to my hips and chest. I examined myself in the mirror, turned myself around to look at my ass. My white underwear created a slight line on the curve of each cheek. My strapless bra created the desired effect on the white sleeveless cotton dress, sprinkled with tiny pink flowers.

I slipped on my suede sandals and pulled out a small white purse that hung in my closet, hardly used. When I stepped into the living room, my mother said, "Wow!"

I had already told her Nicholas was taking me out to brunch.

"I'll be back this afternoon sometime," I said, letting her take in the fact that I was wearing a smidge of make-up, which she always prodded me to wear. I could tell she was proud that such a tiny dress fit me. I looked feminine, which was what she wished for me. This made me both angry and satisfied.

I picked up my keys to leave. We kissed goodbye and I smiled at her as I put on my sunglasses. The bus started up and I waved. Halfway to Sherman Way I realized that I meant to look at the window across the street from my house, wanting the man inside to see me, all dressed up, on my way somewhere.

I imagined Jeff's new apartment as an oasis but for the din of the city that drifted in from his tiny balcony overlooking a parking lot and mini-mall. The apartment complex felt populated yet safe; neighbor's faces were absent, though their movements registered in bumps and overheard television shows, canned laughter and applause beaming through the walls.

Alone. Jeff lived alone now, and I felt it was my influence, the plateau we had reached, where our relationship warranted more time, more privacy, more eye contact and attention to nuance.

I buzzed Jeff's apartment and he answered groggily through the intercom. The door unlocked for me and I headed down the hallway to his front door. I knocked and then opened it without waiting and found him scratching his back, yawning.

I suddenly felt young, overdressed, maybe even ridiculous.

When he took a good look at me, though, I saw something wake up in him and he disappeared into the bathroom to get dressed.

His apartment was a shambles. Boxes still lined the walls and counter space, and only the small black and white television and a stereo were plugged into the outlets. I sat uncomfortably on the sofa and waited for him, jingling my keys.

I was there so he could make good on a favor I did for him. My bus, loaded to the gills, had rumbled back and forth between his previous rental house and this new apartment. "I'll take you out for brunch," Jeff promised as he heaved one last load off the bus, his glasses falling down on his nose. My sandal tapped the carpet as I thought of his promise, and I wondered where we might go.

When Jeff put out his hand, expectant of the keys, I handed them over with a petulant look, silent. As we headed east, bitterness crept into my voice as I answered his questions, until finally I was silent. He asked what was wrong now, and I looked out the window, angry that he didn't trust me to drive, and yet I did not insist. I wondered what kind of lame excuse he'd come up with if we were pulled over.

"Look," Jeff said slowly, staring at the road after minutes of silence, "if you sit through this meal without saying a word, I'm going to throw you off the fucking mountain."

I looked out the window and pouted. My arms were crossed against my chest. *Mountain?* I thought. My lower lip trembled even as I felt my body responding to the anger I incited in him.

He drove us up, up, up until we were in a lot and there were nicely dressed men that wanted to take the bus and park it for us. "Whoa," I said to myself when Jeff opened his door, and I opened mine. People were stepping into the restaurant wearing Sunday dresses, blazers, and high heels. Jeff was in jeans and a shirt. My thighs felt warm in the sun.

"Go inside and get us a table for two," Jeff ordered, and I started walking as he took a ticket from the valet.

Inside there were long tables with white tablecloths, and glass bowls overflowing with fruits and muffins. Men with white aprons and chef's hats stood by and whisked together omelets and frittatas. Crab and shrimp were displayed on ice. Assorted breakfast meats sizzled on tabletop grills and waffles took shape in hot irons.

When we were seated, my eyes lit up. My silence was over.

"I told you this place rocks," Jeff said.

Two plates later, my glass of champagne emptied and refilled countless times, I excused myself to use the bathroom. I looked at the floor as I walked, taking careful steps. I was happy and drunk and my dress felt too short. When I returned, we continued eating, letting the food absorb the alcohol.

A woman with a camera that looked big and out of place approached us, interrupting my drunken ramble. I felt the shudder in my heart, the fear of being found out, accused.

"Would you like your photo taken?" she asked.

I tried not to laugh and stared at Jeff with a puzzled look when he started handing her money. Suddenly he was sitting on my side of the table, his arm around me. Two photos were snapped, and the woman moved onto another table.

When I could only sip at the endless champagne and the plates were cleared, the woman with the camera returned. She handed Jeff two keychains. He handed one to me. I stared down at this keychain in my palm so the sudden inexplicable tears would go back to where they came from before I looked up again.

In the keychain there was a picture of Jeff and I. On the other side was a small square of paper that read "The Castaway," the name of the restaurant. I put it in my purse and looked at Jeff, finally, and I knew I was beaming.

Jeff suggested we move outside to the terrace, and I laughed, thinking, *How could this get any better?* Jeff's hand cradled my elbow as we carried our water glasses out to a table in the sun. I sat down and shook my sandals off. I expected Jeff to give me a look, but he just leaned back in his beautiful patio chair.

"What'll you have? Piña colada? More champagne?"

I eyed his auburn stubble. "Champagne. I guess."

"A double piña colada and a half bottle of champagne," he told the waiter.

We stared out at the Valley, and I realized finally, at the age of sixteen, why it was called the Valley. My legs were crossed and I swung my bare foot in the air. A cigarette sounded delicious after such fine food, with the prospect of more champagne. I said this out loud, knowing the cigarettes were back in the bus.

"Don't go anywhere," Jeff said, and headed off. The word love filled my mouth like a bubble. I leaned back and smiled at the people at other tables. I pondered the Valley laid out below us, the ocean in the distance. We were floating, like the waves of heat off blacktop, only we were just above Burbank on a brown hill. I thought of "Spanish Castle Magic," a Hendrix song I loved, and hummed a few bars.

Jeff returned and handed me my rescued cigarettes. He leaned over and used one hand to cup the tip of the cigarette as he struck a match and lit it. I stared boldly into his eyes as he did this, and his hand lingered on mine for a moment before I took it back to suck hard on the cigarette.

My jaw felt loose and open. I listened to him tell me that he was sick of our arguments, that we were so *beyond* that. He put on his baseball cap and looked up toward the sun.

"It's tough listening to you talk about all your little boyfriends, all the men just lining up at your door, while we have petty arguments and lose our tempers over stupid, inane shit," he said. I stumbled over his words, *men lining up at my door?* My calves were getting hot in the sun and I thought about Nicholas and how he seemed so very far away. I looked out at the Valley to see if I could somehow locate Reseda. I rearranged my legs under the table where there was shade and continued listening, a slight smile playing on my glossed lips.

"I really imagine us having a future together, Wendy," he continued, looking at me and then at his bag of chew on the table. I decided not to give him shit about the tobacco, or the fact that he was using the potted plant next to us as his spittoon. I poured more champagne into my glass.

"So do I," I heard myself say. "I want more than what we have now. I'm worried that our relationship is just based on sex." The anxiety about voicing my feelings had already slithered away like drops of water drying on cement under an angry hot sun.

And still, I held something back. A melancholy settled around my shoulders and I wondered if I was getting sunburnt. I rubbed my nose absently.

"I'm afraid," Jeff began, "but I love you."

I shook my head. I looked behind him at the clear blue sky. No. But yes. But no.

"Yeah, it's true," Jeff continued. We were holding hands across the table and my foot glided along his below. I looked at him and suddenly didn't give a shit that I was drunk and crying.

He repeated the daydreams he'd shared with me off and on throughout our relationship that involved packing up all our stuff, running away together. I nodded, letting him know I imagined the very same things. He ordered me another half bottle of champagne and I wondered if this was a good idea. I felt sick thinking we were drunk, talking this way, that he might not remember the next day. And I suddenly knew.

This conversation would be erased from his memory. By the next day, it might never have occurred.

When we got up to leave, the sun was high west in the sky and I had to hold myself upright with as much energy as I could muster. Jeff drove, which made the most sense under the circumstances. When he stopped at a strange apartment, I didn't protest. He asked me to wait for a few minutes while he went in to buy some weed, and I nodded, wanting to lie down, close my eyes. The bus sat silent in the sun outside the quiet apartment complex.

It's Sunday, I thought to myself. I threw my legs up on the dashboard and let my dress ride up to the top of my thighs. The sun eventually lulled me to sleep.

When we arrived at Jeff's, I rested on his sofa amid all the boxes. He stretched out on the mattress on the floor after opening up the sliding glass balcony door, letting in the breeze. After a while, I got up and drove home. My hair was knotted from the wind. I traipsed in, told my mother I had a great time, went to my room and passed out on the cushions on the floor that served as my bed.

Later, I looked at the souvenir keychain. I have looked at this keychain hundreds of times since.

Jeff has his arm around me and my hair is down, held back with a couple of bobby pins. He is wearing a t-shirt and cap and sporting a beard, smiling, though the way his mouth is placed it looks suspiciously like it contains chewing tobacco. I am looking golden, smiling loosely, white teeth against my tan skin creating a dramatic effect. My long hair covers my neckline. My favorite dress doesn't even show up much in the picture.

The next day Jeff said to me on the phone, "Everything I said yesterday? I meant it all."

The Castaway burned down years later. My mother told me this on the phone. I was a thousand miles away, years from that afternoon, but I remembered it all. And I have the keychain to remind me.

NOTES ON AN EXCAVATION:

EXORCISM

Several relationships in my life have had the difficult and often unspoken task of exorcising Jeff.

Each person deserves a fresh look at their fossil history, a cataloguing of their state of being and their relationship with the flora and fauna—what made them survive, what did not.

There is a story, a book, for each, but they cannot be contained here.

The men with whom I coupled, serial monogamists all, men who found they had to first wrestle with ghosts to get to my core (if they got there):

My sincere apologies.

LATE SUMMER 1989

Whether it was the marijuana or the semblance of having just experienced something I thought unattainable, I floated home many times that summer from Jeff's apartment. Nicholas didn't enter my head until the mornings after, when my journal writing resumed, having left off the previous morning after a secret night with Jeff in his apartment above Denny's. *J. might take me to a blues club*, I wrote in my journal. *Nicholas and I might go out Friday night.*

Arguments with Jeff didn't cease with the presence of those nights. My forehead pulsed with pain after telephone conversations with him when our bickering had us slamming phones or growing silent around each other. I channeled my anger by spending more time with Nicholas, the adventures we had as normal teenagers in the summertime. We camped by the ocean, hiked the hills surrounding the Valley, lugged paper bags of beer and wine up rock croppings and hid from cops in the far reaches of parks after hours.

I sang Nicholas's name to myself, my fingers traced the freckles on his forearms, and my face nuzzled his neck. I looked into his eyes and a tide of guilt swept over me, often, imagining my detours to Jeff's, my journal entries composed of confusion and longing, wondering if it was possible to be in love with two people simultaneously. The tide swept out as I closed my eyes and he kissed me with what I imagined was the purity of a teenage boy.

When I pulled up to my mother's house, I quietly entered and I heard her stir on the living room couch. It was after midnight.

"Wha' time is it?" she said, her voice drunk only with sleep.

"Just after midnight," I whispered, putting my hand on her arm. She raised her eyelids drowsily and said, "I'm so glad you're home," before turning over to face the wall.

Me too, I thought, and tiptoed to my bedroom to open my journal and write.

~

"You're growing up," Jeff said. "That's great. So glad to hear."

I sat on the couch, frozen. I didn't want to look at his face. He issued congratulations and went about his kitchen moving dishes noisily from counter to sink, his voice speeded up, my heart falling away to someplace unreachable.

I had shared with Jeff that I felt *it*. I was falling in love with Nicholas.

"That's great," he repeated, wiping his counters with a fast motion, crumbs slipping off onto the floor. "It must feel really good. Doesn't it?"

I swallowed and looked down at the floor. The carpet was blurry. I let the drops fall on my cheeks.

"So did I tell you about that woman at work?" he asked suddenly. I shook my head without lifting it.

"We totally get along. It's pretty nice, haven't felt that in a while," he continued, scrubbing a dish. He turned the water on full blast and I was grateful for the pause. I was suddenly reeling, wanting time to absorb the new atmosphere in his apartment.

He turned off the sink and looked over at me after some silence. "Shit," he muttered. A tear dropped off the tip of my chin.

"Goddamn it," he said when he sat down next to me. "Goddamn it." I started to shiver. "I'm sorry," he said, "for whatever you're crying about."

A deep red cloud moved in over the place where my heart felt it had been.

"Whatever," I answered.

"Look, Wendy," Jeff began. I heard the shift in his voice, the one that delineated adult from child, teacher from student.

"I've known this for a while. You need to grow up, experience things that have to be experienced by someone your age." He looked at my profile and I studied a stain on the carpet.

"I have to let you go, let you make your mistakes, live your life, so that you're a mature, rounded person. I won't lie, it makes me a little nervous, but it's natural."

"So since you're in love," he began after we sat in silence for some time, "I guess you can't do this." He reached over and squeezed one of my breasts. I pulled away.

"No more nights fucking me senseless in my bed, huh?" he said with a slight smile. "No more quickies in my bathroom, up against the sink, so I can see your face in the mirror while I..."

"Stop it," I said. I stood up, almost losing my balance. "Stop."

"I'm sorry," he said quickly, his face changing. I looked at his face, his slight double chin, the way his hair formed silky ringlets on his head. His glasses were slipping off his nose and he seemed not to notice.

"I'm gonna go," I announced quietly. He stood in the middle of his apartment and watched me. I shut the door behind me and the red cloud moved slightly in my chest. I walked as fast as I could through the corridors of his apartment complex until I reached the safety of outside. I started the ignition of my bus, the chugging and whirring mixed up with my sobbing.

~

My junior year of high school began late in summer. My days were filled with Religion, Government, Psychology, Art History, and Business Law. After school, I raced onto the freeway that would drop me off on the west side of the Valley and knocked timidly on Nicholas's window. He spied me through his window blinds and soon the door opened revealing me in my uniform, my backpack of schoolbooks, jingling car keys.

The warm August nights poured into September. Friday nights I gave Nicholas's friends rides to his house, where we could expect to drink beer in his small bedroom, or we walked over to John's garage for some manner of getting wasted mixed with improvised band practice.

We hiked up Stony Point one night. Our party of eight people cursed, called out drunkenly into the night, slipped on rocks and laughed with each other. Nicholas forged ahead both up and down the primitive peak while I followed the backs of his friends, carefully estimating my footing and wishing I hadn't drank any Strawberry Hill at the top of the rock.

"Wendy's doing okay," he said when one of his friends asked why he wasn't helping me down the face of the rocks. I felt my neck hairs bristle and my mouth tighten.

"Yeah, Wendy's a trooper," his friend agreed. My mouth untwisted and I stopped for a moment, leaning against the flat surface of a jutting rock.

I had somehow transformed into the responsible girlfriend, the only one who was still in school and got report cards, had a driver's license and a car. My bus became a shuttle for nineteen and twenty-year-old boys that wanted to drink Jack Daniels mixed with Big Gulp cups full of Coke from 7-11 and play their instruments in a dark, musty garage outfitted with carpets, amateur soundproofed walls.

~

"I'm gonna go outside and have a smoke," I said to Jeff. It had been a month since I'd last seen him. I stood up from his couch and grabbed my bag.

"Just smoke it in here," Jeff said. I raised my eyebrows. He opened the balcony door and gave me a clean ashtray I'd never seen before.

"You haven't been coming over as often," Jeff said after I finished half my cigarette in silence. "I guess you're busy with what's-his-name."

I sucked in my cheeks and stubbed out my cigarette.

"I guess you could say that," I answered. "And I'm trying to stay on top of school."

"Ahh," Jeff said, nodding. A dimple appeared in one cheek when he gave me a slight smile. "I like to hear that."

"Just two more years," I said, looking out the window at the Denny's parking lot.

"Just two more years," Jeff agreed. "Doesn't stop me from wanting to fuck you now."

I turned and looked at him. His words sounded crass and un-called for in a way they never sounded to me before.

After he remarked a few more times that I was avoiding his apartment and how that hurt him, I felt the fingers of guilt close around me. I made an excuse and left soon after, even though it was a bright Sunday afternoon and school was still hours and hours away.

SEPTEMBER 1989

"Happy birthday," I said into the intercom.

"Oh, yeah," Jeff answered, his voice thick with sleep. "C'mon up." He buzzed me in and I walked the hallways to his door.

When he greeted me, I snuck a look over his shoulder. Clothes were strewn on the floor, dishes in piles on the counter. I hid his birthday gift under my arm and he ushered me in.

"Jesse's coming over in a bit," he said, straightening up the apartment. "We're going to a baseball game."

"Oh," I said, watching him. "I'm going camping with Nicholas. We're leaving this afternoon."

Moments later Jesse called out over the intercom and Jeff buzzed him in. Jeff was pulling on a baseball cap when Jesse bounded down the hall and opened the door.

"Oh, I have this for you," I said suddenly after Jesse gave me a friendly hello. I handed Jeff the paper bag. Inside was the book *One* by Richard Bach. Jeff opened the front cover and read my inscription, which spoke benignly of friendship. He looked at me. I saw something shift in his face and suddenly wished Jesse wasn't in the room.

"I love it," Jeff said. "You're the only one who knows what I really like, Wendy. You always write the nicest things for me on my birthday." He crossed over to me and surprised me with an embrace.

"Hey, do I get one?" Jesse joked, and I pulled back from Jeff, my face reddening, wishing it was night, wishing our plans were different.

Jesse told Jeff he'd wait out front in his car for him. Alone, Jeff turned to me.

"Why don't we just stay here all day and read it in bed?"

I smiled, silent.

"I know, I know," Jeff said in mock apologetic tones. "You have a boyfriend and a life." He tossed the book onto his mattress. "But someday he'll be gone. You'll be writing the books, I'll be reading them." I pressed my lips together and stared into his eyes.

"Sure you can't make it to the game with us?" he asked when we were walking down the apartment hallway.

I started to say something about camping and he turned and hugged me. I held on until he said, "Well, if you decide not to go, I have my own special present to give to you, so stop by."

We had one last embrace on the sidewalk as Jesse's engine hummed. *I don't want to write any more because I may be doubtful of some things and sure of others...so farewell for now*, I wrote in my journal later that afternoon before I threw my backpack in the bus and headed out to Nicholas and to the coastal highway where the ocean was a stone's throw from my open, sun-warmed hands.

FALL
1989

From five p.m. to nine p.m. Monday through Thursday, I walked the dimming autumn streets of the Valley, knocking on doors and offering subscriptions to the *Los Angeles Times*.

A group of us, ranging in age from sixteen to sixty-something, were shuttled in the company van by a friendly but firm taskmaster who frequently chided us for selling too few subscriptions. I stopped paying attention to him when he offered any one of us twenty-five dollars if we could come up with a good vanity plate for his new sports car. He had already tried 55 SUX, and the Department of Motor Vehicles denied him, so it was up to our crew to come up with the winning plate. I looked out the window trying not to roll my eyes as we drove through Van Nuys, Sepulveda, and Reseda.

I told my mother I was telemarketing in an office, hawking the L.A. Times. She looked closely at me and I looked away at the stack of free souvenir books I carried, one gift per customer that subscribed.

"Why do you have those?" she asked, her chin nodding in the direction of the shiny, softcover volumes.

"I send 'em to people when I make a sale," I lied.

Jeremy, a longtime seller and clearly the boss's favorite, was instructed to accompany me on my first week, and he offered himself as an escort thereafter, especially when our supervisor pointed out that I was the only girl in the crew, not counting Hildy, our sixty-something seller, who carried a flask in her purse. I cruised neighborhoods with Jeremy who struck down all the stereotypes I had of the favorite employee. He was seventeen, a heavy metal fan, had long feathered hair and liked to party.

But work still came first. Awestruck at Jeremy's ability to talk anyone into subscribing, I clammed up, feeling certain that selling was most definitely not one of my strong points. When potential customers invited us in for a smoke while Jeremy went on his spiel about current events and classifieds and daily movie listings, we leisurely entered their living rooms and Jeremy made the sales final. More often than not, the customers even offered us joints, or a hit from a water pipe, and Jeremy and I slapped hands in victory as we made our way down the street to the next apartment complex, high as kites.

When I sold only two subscriptions in an evening, Jeremy nonchalantly dropped a few of his subscriber cards next to my leg as we sat on a sidewalk for a spell.

"Really?" I asked.

He shrugged. "But practice your technique," he added.

"I know, I know," I said. "It's just hard to do when you're high."

He looked at me blankly, his brown feathered hair falling against his clean-shaven cheeks. I knew he did not share the feeling.

It was after eleven one Friday night. School and work had me exhausted, stretched out and dozing on the floor after snapping a quick bongload in my bedroom, incense burning to mask the smell. The phone rang and my body shot up to answer it before my mother could pick up the kitchen extension.

"Jeez, you're alive?" Jeff said into my ear when I mumbled a hello.

"Yep," I said, stretching out with the phone to my ear. I pushed away a pile of books and rested my head on my arm.

"I haven't seen or heard from you in ages. I wondered if you were dead," he said.

"Nope," I answered. I peered down at my belly and watched it slowly rise and fall.

"Well, sounds like you're beat," Jeff said. He sounded alert and wanting to talk. "Stop by tomorrow if you want. I'll be home all day grading papers."

"Okay," I answered, my eyes closing. I hung up the phone. I turned and lied on my back, my head hitting the edge of the answering machine. Dead? I was running around, alive, between Nicholas's, John's garage, and Notre Dame High School, while also selling subscriptions all over the Valley.

Alive, running, I thought as I softly entered sleep again. *But where?*

≈

As Thanksgiving vacation approached, my report card reflected the best grades I'd had since beginning high school. The report card was passed from my mother's hands to my grandmother's, and money was passed to mine. I was pulling in the minimum required subscription sales for the Times and scoring more than my fair share of joints and bong hits from generous and kind men and women across the Valley. I gave away the premium gifts when someone couldn't afford a subscription but shared their marijuana. The pile of glossy picture books dwindled, and my mother stopped asking questions about my "telemarketing" job.

My paychecks and commission money bought dime bags and car insurance payments, fast food on the way home from Nicholas's and Victoria's Secret lingerie. The bus was still breaking down regularly. Extra commission money funded the resurrection of my bus in auto shops where it was perpetually being towed.

I was sixteen and a half and could see the time crunch in my schedule from studying, working nights, and playing weekends. Nicholas's attentions were shared equally between me, his band practice, his sometime odd jobs, and drinking. Nights at John's garage could go by without ten words between us, and after a bottle of Boone's Farm, I felt justified in walking out, slamming the door and starting the ignition of my bus and taking off with as much dramatics as I could muster. Thus began the interminable discussions, slurred and messy, where I questioned Nicholas's commitment to me and refused to give his friends rides anywhere. I ranted from the driver's seat, Nicholas held his head down and answered me quietly from the passenger's seat. The scene became a ritual we wouldn't break from for a long, long time.

One night after such a discussion, I refused his friend Junky a ride home and denied Nicholas a night with me in his bed. I had the particular intention to stop by Jeff's apartment on my way home.

The moon was high and white, round and perfect in the sky. I drove swiftly through the streets, my rationalizations increasing with each stoplight. *It's boring as hell at John's garage. Nicholas is drunk most of the time. We're never alone anymore, his friends are always around. Drunk as usual.* When Jeff's apartment was on the horizon, the voices dulled into nothing, replaced by a warm feeling lower than my stomach, creating heat in my fingertips.

Two hours passed slowly in his apartment.

"Beautiful," he whispered at me over and over. "You're getting so beautiful."

The moonlight drifted in from behind the sheet on the balcony door. In its path I saw my clothes, slipped off as if in a spell, a random lighter on the rug, one of Jeff's belts.

After, I closed my eyes and felt his heavy hand on my hip.

"So are you going to spend the night?" he whispered into my hair. My eyes flew open.

"No, no, forget it," he said quickly. "Before I could get you again in the morning, the cops'd be banging on my door."

I didn't want to hear words anymore. He had spent the first half hour of my clandestine visit telling me that he finally felt like he could reasonably go out and meet women.

"I'll either wait for one to turn legal," he said, pointing a finger at my chest, "or I'll meet someone sooner or later who is."

NOTES ON AN EXCAVATION:

2007–2010

For nearly three years I met a Jungian analyst weekly, then twice weekly, in an office of West Los Angeles.

One of the times we met, she said, "It seems as though your natural state is one of hiding, secrets, shame; it is where you possibly feel most comfortable. From the moment you began hiding your parents' alcoholism from others," she explained, "you drew the cloak of secrets and shame around your shoulders so that it became something you would wear, always."

I listened to her and tried to let the image sink in.

It was only until she said she had tremendous empathy for the child I was, the girl who so early on felt the need to take on secrets, to lie and hide for the sake of other people, to protect them, did I begin to feel the import.

It was then that the numbness was punctured and I started to cry.

The veil had been pulled back for a moment on all the situations I had participated in after Jeff. There were the infidelities, always preceding breakups with boyfriends and the periods of stable, pleasant and even fulfilling relationships I exchanged for thick lust with someone else, like a smoke I could, and did, get lost in. For as long as I could remember, there were the secrets I found myself weaving with a lover or potential lover, man or woman, the co-conspiratorial air that forced such strange intimacy.

"Secret-keeping. It's what you know, what you've become used to, starting with your family," my analyst told me. "It's your inheritance."

Sometimes I still have to find my way out of the smoke, to touch what is real, to confirm what is illusion.

I want to relinquish this inheritance.

1990

1990

I approached seventeen with a job at a drugstore, a job that offered full-time hours in summer, which I negotiated into four ten-hour days for the sake of long weekends where I wouldn't have to dress in the scratchy brown polyester uniform. I scooped runny mounds of rocky road ice cream in sugar cones, rang up hemorrhoid cream, baking soda, or tire cleaner at the register, accepted film developing orders, and screened papers cut from prescription pads from all manner of people as the pharmacist filled orders. Smoking pot was tempered by my weekly shifts at Thrifty's Drugstore, and my free time seemed to contract to the size of a pinhole that I filled with Nicholas and our hobbies: drinking, going to rock concerts, having sex in his bedroom.

Internally, I fought constantly with the word *love*.

I'd been using it freely for some time, whispering it in Nicholas's ear, writing it in letters that he unfolded and read standing up in his bedroom, a slight smile on his face. Sitting in his friend's apartment or another friend's backyard, I smoldered with resentment when I took the backseat to cases of beer, talk of muscle cars, or band practice that always sounded lousy anyway. As the band played their version of the Rolling Stones song "Bitch," I got up and left, as I always did, without a word, *love* slipping from my grasp, bitterness replacing it.

Senior year began and my days shortened at school. Working more hours, confined in the brown polyester uniform, I thought of Jeff intermittently, like when an older man came in to fill a prescription for Zantac. I remembered Jeff tossing the pills into his hand and throwing them back with water or a beer. I never understood what he took them for. At the pharmacy I rang up boxes of condoms for women in their twenties, and considered Jeff and his disdain for condoms. When my male co-workers looked through the thick photo envelopes belonging to attractive young female customers, I thought of Jeff. We hadn't made contact in months, and from our last phone call, I knew he was sharing an apartment now, with an older female landlord he proclaimed to hate.

One night, my phone rang and Nicholas announced himself. He was at a friend's house, wasted, and wanted to know if I could come out to pick him up.

"Nope," I answered, stretching out on my makeshift bed. The mattress and bed frame had long been replaced by the foldable cushion I slept on. I liked this cushion, because it felt portable, simple, and close to the floor, where I liked to sit or stretch. I hung up the phone.

Minutes later the phone rang again and I picked it up, my eyes rolling in disgust. It was Jeff. His speech was slurred. I imagined empty beer cans and the scent of bong water.

"So are you and Nicholas still a thing?" he asked. "Am I still on your list?"

My free hand tightened into a fist.

"You know," I began, "I don't like the fact that you only call me, drunk no less, to ask me questions like that." My thumb rubbed my knuckles, and my forehead tensed.

"When I do see you, you dance around the issue of you and me, but when you're drunk, you think nothing of calling me and confronting me in a gross way." My fist relaxed, my palm hot. I set it gently on my belly.

"First of all," Jeff hissed, "for your information, I'm not drunk. It's the medication I'm on. Second of all, your accusations are insulting. I don't really give a fuck how Nicholas is doing, but it's something to say. It's called a *nicety.*

"I don't hear from you for a fuck of a long time, and when I call, you lay into me, assuming I can only be drunk to dial your number, and you doubt me from the moment I start talking. What the fuck kind of friendship is that?" he bellowed.

I was silent as he hammered the same point over and over, seeming to get increasingly excited by the sheer ludicrousness of this situation he found himself in and my alleged overreaction.

The tears dried on my face. I breathed into the phone as he continued. A numbness I was long used to overwhelmed my body.

"I love you, Wendy Ortiz. I, Jeff Ivers, of Van Nuys, California, love you, and all you can do is lay into me for calling you drunk, which I'm not," he said emphatically into my ear. "I'm not dating anyone, I'm not chasing any women around because I don't want that other shit, I want you."

"I have loved you from the moment I first talked to you. Do you believe that? Think I'm lying, that I'm just drunk? Well, fuck you. I dug you from the moment I saw you. What's wrong with me seeing a future for us? You may not know this, you may write me off as a drunk old man, but I'd marry you tomorrow if I could. *Tomorrow.*"

A powerful nausea crept into my gut and I was no longer numb. My body was still, immobile with uncertainty.

I kept listening as he detailed the old fantasies of he and I, the dredged-up images of some kind of future together. I listened with a tired heart. I listened with an ear that felt like fire, my hands busy flexing, trying to grasp something, anything that might make sense.

1991

SUMMER
1991

We didn't speak again until I was eighteen, a month graduated from high school.

I was a young woman of legal age, the age we had always talked about, imagined.

I stood in his living room, a different house across the valley, the furthest away Jeff ever lived from me since we'd started seeing each other.

He greeted me jovially, introduced me to his cousin from whom he was renting a room. He ushered me into his bedroom, where a wrapped gift sat in the middle of the bed, along with a card hidden in an envelope.

"You look great," Jeff said. "What's it been? Six months?"

"Mmhm," I answered, sitting awkwardly on the edge of his bed. His eyes scanned my white jeans, my form-fitting white shirt, the black belt with its peace sign buckle. I crossed one leg over the other and wondered where he had been during my graduation. I knew not to ask.

"Here," he said, leaning close to me. He picked up the gift and the envelope and placed them in my lap. I laughed, anxious, and bit my bottom lip.

The card was peppered with his small, messy writing. I looked closely and discovered that he had transcribed the lyrics of a song into the body of the card. I read the words quickly, skin goosebumping as he stared at me.

"Wow," I said, looking up at him. He smiled and sat down next to me.

"'Fortress Around My Heart.' I think of you every time I hear it." He looked down at the wrapped gift in my lap. "Go ahead," he said.

I unwrapped the gift, discovering a box underneath the paper. I pried it open and gingerly pulled out the contents.

"It's a Tiffany," Jeff said as I held up the stained glass. The scene was of a river, rolling hills, blue sky. "We're those rivers, remember, the way they meet the sea."

A lump in my throat formed and I put the stained glass back in the box.

"Can I hug you?" I said.

"You bet," he answered. We stood and hugged.

"One more thing," he said, reaching into his back pocket. He handed me two tickets.

The tickets were for the blues show he'd told me about that happened every summer. I threw myself at him joyfully, letting my body press into his momentarily before pulling away. We sat down again and made plans to go to the show in his new car the following weekend. I left soon after, the stained glass on the floor of the bus as I drove Roscoe Boulevard from one end of the valley to the other, my hands tapping the steering wheel excitedly.

∼

My knees were bent, elbows resting on them as I stared out at the stage.

There was a grassy incline, at least fifty rows of seats and some cement between me and the bass that was being plucked, the voice stretched like silk across all the bodies until it reached my ears.

I rubbed the undersides of my thighs where the grass had crept and stuck to my skin. My periwinkle blue and white jumper only reached mid-thigh, and I considered retrieving my sweater from the rumpled backpack at my side. I glanced over at Jeff. He was lying on his side, drifting in and out of the current of music, watching me. We couldn't stop smiling at each other. I looked back at the stage. I conjured up Nicholas in my head, how he expected me to be home that evening after the day-long blues festival, how he didn't know which friend I had gone with, how we had tentative plans to hang out in Louise Park alone for once, without the annoyance of his friends ruining the evening.

I had already heard Jeff squawk at the fact that I made a date for after the show; when I looked away from him and sighed, he understood it was a moot point.

I laughed and shrieked excitedly on the drive to the amphitheater. Jeff's new car reminded me of the cars I watched out for in the streets of the Valley, the ones we presumed were undercover cops. I sat in the spacious passenger seat and bounced under my seat belt, looking this way and that, pleased to be riding with him to the blues show.

We went through a drive-through and got back on the main road with a tray of nachos and a bag of soft tacos. We found a free spot in a sea of cars in the enormous venue parking lot. The afternoon sun was still high and we rolled down our windows. I tuned the radio and we opened up the bags and picked at the square-shaped box of nachos hungrily.

"What a perfect day," Jeff said, wiping away red sauce from his mouth. I followed his eyes out past the windshield. A group of women, by all appearances in their thirties, walked by carrying foldable chairs and a small cooler. I noted how his eyes scanned their legs, their asses, the reaches of hair falling down their backs. I snapped my fingers by his ear and laughed. His head jumped back with exaggeration.

"Caught you," I said. He proclaimed his innocence and I turned in my seat to face him, laughing between accusations.

"You were totally looking at their asses, Jeff," I said, dipping a chip into a small plastic tray of cheese. "I saw it all." I was not the headliner anymore and I could watch him watch women and not feel a thing, except that he was a chauvinist and probably wouldn't change. I laughed out loud.

"Yeah. Like my eyes could stray far from *your* little outfit," he said, taking another bite of his taco. My knee jerked and the tray of nachos spilled over, little gobs of cheese transplanted to his new car upholstery. I shrieked and dove for napkins in the fast-food bag.

≈

It was cool and relaxed on the lawn at the blues show. Everyone was friendly and smiling and Jeff shared a joint he brought with me and a man and woman nearby. They were sitting on a pastel-colored blanket and sipping at wine coolers bought from the concession stands. Jeff nodded at one.

"Want me to go get you one?"

I nodded and my eyes followed him as he bent a knee against the grass, pushed himself up, and stood over me.

"Don't run away now," he joked, and pushed his glasses up on his nose. I knew that he noticed every man who had turned in my direction. His response was to lean closer to me or look me in the eye and shake his head like he couldn't believe their rudeness.

My eyes followed the crowd, the bobbing heads, the walking forms of people who were safely in their adulthood. I swallowed and willed myself to take deep breaths, aware that I was young here, alone. I figured it would be awhile before Jeff got back to our safe patch of grass.

I was alone in a sea of adults who presumably loved the blues. I knew we were waiting patiently for the finale, the genius of B.B. King to take the stage.

This was the umpteenth concert of my young life, and light years different from what I was used to at concerts. Everyone had a semblance of calm and happiness, a contentment that felt like milk over hot skin, soothing and exciting at once. My thighs felt cold, and I remembered that that morning I hated the flesh, wished my thighs smaller. I tapped a bare foot against the grass and watched the sinking sun.

Before I made it to Nicholas's that evening, I endured countless pinpricks of innuendo that Jeff shot, beginning with his eyes on me, his mouthing of words, I want you, and his belief, stated several times, that a successful blues concert experience must end in passionate lovemaking at his place. I hid my every response under a semblance of amusement even as I imagined what the night might hold.

I tilted my head at him as we sat in his car, waiting for the long line of brake lights to let up and coast away slowly. His mouth was slightly open, anticipating an opening in the line of vehicles and I thought of his teeth, the feel of my tongue in the gap between them. I felt a strange sense of endearment, a bizarre and new feeling of wanting to protect him.

I covered my legs with my backpack and lay my head against the tan headrest. He let me smoke a cigarette with the window rolled down and I wondered, suddenly, how we would say goodbye.

FALL
1991

Two months after the blues concert, I leaned against the wooden frame of an abandoned lifeguard post. Jeff and I had climbed onto one of the platforms. My body felt strange around him now, our visits becoming rarer. Every time I saw him it was necessary to ease back into our relationship, over and over.

An airplane blipped across the sky and the stars struggled to be seen. I turned to look behind us. Across the Pacific Coast Highway and up, houses sat, seemingly safe on their foundations. Each home was well-lit, warm-looking. I shivered and leaned back into the wood.

Jeff saw me looking at the houses.

"Wouldn't it be great? Living up there?"

I nodded, watching the waves softly thrash the sand. I felt mute, unsure of what was safe to express and what was not. My calves ached from standing on my feet all day at work. I had dropped plans with Nicholas to come out to the ocean with Jeff. Something about the invitation felt final, last ditch.

I met him at his house and he drove us in his car through the canyons, down to the coastal highway. We parked and talked, walked out onto the sand, and found our way to the lifeguard post.

"I can imagine us in a place like that," Jeff began. I sighed and looked him in the eye.

He put his hand on mine. My mind flashed on Nicholas.

"I'm not sure you are ever going to get just how I love you." His hand moved up my arm and suddenly my body responded, inching closer to his, until his arms were around me, and my arms circled his neck, his shoulder. We held each other in silence and I felt my heart beating through my chest, as if it wanted to live outside my body.

After one kiss, I sat back and set my eyes on the waves again. The water lapped away from the sand as if in fast motion reverse. I wished for a way to reverse so many things, to push a button and rewind. Jeff left an arm around my shoulder and I pressed into it, leaning my head back to look into the sky. The crescent moon sat mute.

On my way home from Jeff's house, I stopped at Nicholas's. He let me in after I rapped my knuckles on his window. His face showed signs of sleep.

I wanted this thing with Jeff to be over, truly over. I wanted to have one less secret, to have a regular relationship with someone, to see what might happen to the regular relationship I was already in with Nicholas. To punctuate the decision, I decided to come clean about where I had been that night, how it was the last time.

Nicholas had known about Jeff, not from my telling, but second-hand, years before, from Abigail. It had been the cause of one of our many break-ups. And then he had assumed, with my assurance, that the relationship had not continued.

To Nicholas, my revelation was like a footnote to an old story.

He held me. I smelled his flannel shirt and wondered about what I had just done.

"I understand," he whispered into my hair. "I still love you. You did what you needed to do."

Waves of guilt, resignation, fear, and love, washed through me as I clutched his flannel, wanting to be sure of this person who could love and forgive, who could scare me with his understanding. I was telling him what I could not tell so many others. My closest friends had known the gist, and one had even questioned Jeff and his motivations, but I'd shrugged it off, stopped talking about it. Now here I was with Nicholas, waiting for a break-up but receiving, instead, understanding.

I sat on his bed for a long time after, watching him as he slept, his eyelids fluttering softly, his blonde curls on the pillow. I picked up my keys from his night table, clenched them to keep from making noise, and stole away from his house to head home.

LATE FALL
1991

Another three months passed before I saw Jeff again.

The leaves had fallen from the trees, brown and crackled under my shoes. I was enrolled at community college, watching films in darkened classrooms and reading film theory, struggling through college algebra, producing weekly essays I received steady A's for in English composition.

We met near Ventura Boulevard one night and I parked my car on the street. The meters were switched off. A chilly wind swept a plastic bag down the sidewalk as I approached Jeff's car. He leaned over to unlock the door for me and I got in.

"Why're you in the station wagon?" he asked, looking through the rearview mirror.

"Why do you think? That fucking bus..."

Soon he was turning the steering wheel this way and that through the hills demarcating Hollywood from the Valley. I tried to follow his navigation, as I had started driving the hills over to Hollywood every Sunday night to dance at Club 1970. I lost track of the turns he took off the main road. We came to a stop on a dusty, dead end street.

The nearby houses were dark and Jeff turned the radio up until I could make out the voices. I was reminded of years before, being parked on a similar road, begging for kisses, wanting the night to stretch out until it ended with him in love with me; and me, older and presumably mature, ready for whatever could happen next.

We talked about college, the classes that I'd chosen, and my decision to focus on English literature and political science. He nodded at me, smiling as I spoke, and I could feel the weight my voice seemed to carry. I had his attention in a different way I couldn't yet identify.

I listened to him talk about his new job at another private school. I watched his face as he spoke, the gap between his teeth, his glasses, the red in his cheeks and his combed black hair, short and neat for this new school. When he spoke of a woman he thought he was falling in love with, a woman he worked with at the new school, I tried to smile. I remembered the sick feeling I had when he congratulated me for falling in love with Nicholas.

I smiled, nodded. "Wow. I'm glad for you."

We looked out the windshield at the night, the hanging eucalyptus trees.

"You need to be out in the world, experiencing things," he said. "I'm going to let you go so you can do that. It's only right. The rivers will always meet the sea, Wendy, so I'm doing this for our own good."

An itch of annoyance sprang up in me. I knew enough not to corrupt the moment with questions. The itchiness accompanied an awareness that his words were empty of meaning. The river. The sea. Whatever. I wondered over the years of pronouncements, the declarations of love, the accusations and unspoken scenes that we played out. They finally smoothed out into an uncomplicated silence, the ripples of questions and confusion suddenly flat and quiet.

I stared through the windshield trying to make out shapes in the dark. I closed my eyes shut, trying to maintain the smooth emptiness, the flat dimensions of darkness that flooded my view from the inside of the car. My throat unclenched and I heard a sound come from me. I wished it back but suddenly Jeff was holding me, his voice broken, his face buried in my chest. I let my hands touch his hair, his warm neck, stroking, knowing this would be the last time.

This was it.

"I love you, Wendy," he said into my chest, his voice cracking.

"I love you, too," I said.

He pulled back and looked at me.

"I love you."

"I love you," I repeated back.

His eyes were the whole world. I felt like I could save the form of his body in my hands somehow, forever.

When we pulled away from each other, I bit my tongue and my hands felt empty. We listened to the music on the radio in silence until he started the car without a word and we wound our way down into the Valley again, the turns and twists wringing my insides, my mouth suddenly dry.

The secret, my secret, what I had never allowed myself to say, was out.

It hung in the air above us, the complexity of it, the impossibility of it, the darkness and corruptness of it, never to be spoken of in one another's presence again.

NOTES ON AN EXCAVATION:

PRESENT DAY FINDS

In the first few months of my daughter's life, our usual stroller walk took us in and around La Brea Tar Pits. Our apartment was less than a mile from the grounds and it seemed the most scenic destination within walking distance.

When you approach the tar pits from the southwest corner of Wilshire Boulevard and Curson Avenue, you are immediately hit with the overwhelming smell of pitch. Caution tape and fluorescent-striped sandwich boards redirect your steps away from a bubbling puddle of liquid asphalt. You cross the street and walk under an archway and there they are. On a breezy day the palm trees clatter. The sound of traffic on Wilshire is lulling. If you lived in Los Angeles as a child, you may have come here to learn about dinosaurs. If you live in Los Angeles as an adult, you come because of its proximity to an art museum and a natural history museum, and because it's a pleasant walk.

~

I pushed the stroller and contemplated the sludge. I'm always surprised to hear the goo gurgling, the reminder that this is living material, thriving with bacteria and whatever random plant or animal it sucks up and preserves in its liquid body.

Overcoming the countless fears that popped into my head on an hourly basis, I pushed her stroller through the park several times a week. I wondered if the stench of tar was enough to sicken her. I wondered if it was toxic to be breathing it in so often. I didn't pay attention to the life-sized mammoths. For the first few months I could only take in so much.

Gone were my usual television cravings for repeat episodes of *Law & Order: SVU*. Instead I found myself capable of watching romantic comedies, a genre I usually loathed. And yet the shock of a newborn suddenly made me frantic to push past any channel that featured horror, abduction, violence or anything resembling any kind of chaotic scene or situation. I could only consume the lightest, fluffiest of television. Sleep deprivation and constant nursing kept me awake at all hours. The need to feel pinned down to a soft, uncomplicated reality kept me in front of the television.

Even once I was past that phase and started getting more sleep, there were the little fears, the ones that come with caring for a tiny person who is completely dependent on you.

As I pushed the stroller through Hancock Park and out to the grounds of the Los Angeles County Museum of Art, I considered looking up on the Internet whether it was safe to be breathing this air we shared with the tar pits.

As a mother I have tried with every fiber of my being to not become what I grew up with—the mother and grandmother who worried constantly, trying to suffocate me with their projections of what could go wrong, often learned through television and movies that depicted unthinkable acts perpetrated on women.

And yet I had undergone unthinkable acts right under the noses, Perhaps they had suspected. And yet nothing had been done.

Now, with a daughter of my own, I like to imagine I'll be able to counter every untruth she might try to pull on me when she's a teenager, that I will be three steps ahead of her, consulting my own catalog of experiences to be able to cut her off at the dangerous pass she wants to take. My worries are magnified by my own experience of women who claim to love you and want to protect you and yet can't seem to, don't know how to. I like to believe I know something different, will rise to whatever circumstance is given me.

But of course I want nothing like what happened in my life to happen in hers. To even come close to happening. I want a magical existence for her, one without pain, illness, sadness. I know this is impossible but I still want it. There are always those impossible things we still want, aren't there?

~

I could never have imagined the life I have now back then.

I did not run away to Montana with an older man. I did run to the Pacific Northwest for eight years. I did fall in love and out of love and in love and out of love again. Introduced to intuition and how to catalog my own insights, I was able to start looking back at that fossilized time and understand, make correlations, write the history. The history I write is just one prism of a history, a place where a part of me feels trapped in time. In my ancient history, a man arrived as my junior high teacher and metamorphosed into someone I would timidly think of as my lover.

The fossils of a woman have been found in the La Brea Tar Pits. The "La Brea Woman" is about 10,000 years old. The La Brea

Woman is thought to have been between the ages of 17-25 when she died. Someone unearthed her, freed her body from the bitumen. I watch people holding the black fence that keeps them from losing themselves in the lake of muck. We do not want to become a part of the ooze primordial. An ooze that lives on. An ooze that emits bubbles on its surface to this day, bubbles created by bacteria that eat the petroleum and release the methane gas. This bacteria is thought to be composed of somewhere in the range of 200-300 previously unknown species. I imagine a microscopic orgy of mystery paisleys cavorting in the black, coloring the oil slicks.

We are talking about alchemical processes. "Destructive distillation," in which living things decomposing are heated to high temperatures in the midst of little to no oxygen. Natural deposits, rich in matter that is, in altered forms, considered worthy of value. Worthy of wars, even.

My own composition was changed when I met and was taught by this man. He seeped into my existence. I smelled the danger and for many reasons, I wandered in.

Could anyone, anything, have saved me?

The bubbles form, pop the surface. The bubbles fill my computer screen when it sits ten minutes idle, my head suddenly a fog detached from my body, a pleasant but sinister dissociation occurring.

The current era: I live in my home city of Los Angeles. After several years of struggling with an unnamed something, I gave it a name and its name turned out to be queerness.

The sense of belonging I feel in the family I have created is unlike any other feeling I've ever had. I belong to this tribe, this small tribe living in a modified Craftsman bungalow in West Adams near a freeway. The freeway and its sound of ocean just like when I was growing up next to one.

The woman I love is . . . a woman. It would take me getting married to a man to remember who I was before.

The woman I love, at times, especially early in our relationship, reminded me of Jeff. I told her so. We understand this as a bizarre and even slightly disturbing outcome, but here we are.

Her charm, her easygoing way of talking to people—the way acquaintances of hers and mine gush to me how much they like her, how hard she works, how sweet, charming, funny she is—all of these claims were once made to me, around me, about Jeff.

In this era, she is a woman who is mere months older than me. We may have had an intense start—both of us ending long committed relationships—but here we are. We remain.

We walk among the palms and the grasses and the fences at Hancock Park. We are a tight little family, we and the daughter we planned for and conceived together. The two of them walk toward the trail that will lead them to the art museum. I linger by the placard describing the asphalt seeps, the fiberglass models of these prehistoric animals that replicate what has been found underneath.

We are walking on fossils daily.

The La Brea Woman is long dead but lives on in a display, along with a variety of creatures. They perished in the tar that also preserved them.

The display is how we tell this story.

Let me excavate. Brush this bone off.

Let me know its story.

ACKNOWLEDGMENTS

Deep gratitude to Kevin Sampsell and Future Tense Books. I got to have the experience many people wish for: a publisher located my work online, commented, then struck up a conversation with me about what else I was working on. And now we have this book. Major thanks to Tina Morgan, editor extraordinaire.

For having read and given insightful feedback on early versions of this book since its very first draft in 2000, I thank Bernard Cooper, Paul Lisicky, David Ulin, Emily Rapp, and Hazel Kight Witham.

For over a dozen years of cheerleading, love and support, I thank fellow writer Karrie Higgins.

Sarah Buller, thank you for being the one person who made me think differently about this chapter of my life at the tender age of sixteen.

Massive love to Sandy Lee, for everything. Everything.

Author Photo: Meiko Takechi Arquillos

Wendy C. Ortiz is a writer born and raised in Los Angeles. She wrote a year-long, monthly column for *McSweeney's Internet Tendency*, and her work has appeared in *The New York Times*, *Vol. 1 Brooklyn*, *The Nervous Breakdown*, *The Rumpus*, and many other journals. She was a writer-in-residence at Hedgebrook, a rural retreat for women writers, in 2007 and 2009. She co-founded the Rhapsodomancy Reading Series in 2004 and has curated and hosted since. Wendy is a parent, an adjunct faculty in creative writing, and sees clients in private practice as a registered marriage and family therapist intern.

Visit her at www.wendyortiz.com.

CPSIA information can be obtained
at www.ICGtesting.com
Printed in the USA
BVHW081934300620
582602BV00003B/218